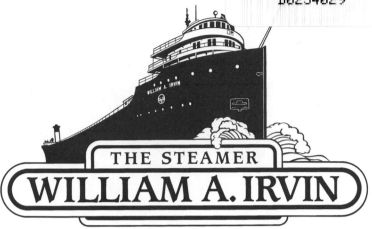

THE STEAMER
WILLIAM A. IRVIN

"The Queen of the Silver Stackers"

by Jody Aho

Copyright 1995
by Avery Color Studios, Inc.

Published by Avery Color Studios, Inc.
Gwinn, Michigan 49841

ISBN #0-932212-85-9
Library of Congress Card No. 95-078442

July, 1995
Reprinted 2000

William A. Irvin and his wife, Gertrude, at the November 10, 1937 launch-ing of the WILLIAM A. IRVIN. (Duluth Entertainment Convention Center collection)

Acknowledgements

When I started working on this book nearly a year ago, I had no idea that I would learn as much about the WILLIAM A. IRVIN or that I would require the assistance of so many people—many of whom I've known for years, others of whom I've known only through a phone conversation. My goal has been to create a book designed for two different audiences—first, the reader who has little knowledge of Great Lakes shipping and, in most cases, touring the IRVIN was his or her first time aboard any ship; and second, the reader who has an avid interest in Great Lakes shipping and whose bookcase, like mine, is filled with books pertaining to Great Lakes shipping and the ships that sail (and have sailed) the Lakes. Without those who have helped me throughout the project, this book would not have become possible. I wish to thank the following for their generous contributions.

First, I wish to thank Dennis Medjo, IRVIN director, who gave me the initial idea for the book, who arranged for me to use his office in the Duluth Entertainment Convention Center to enter the manuscript into the computer, and who helped me through the lengthy process of getting the book published (it has been a learning experience for both of us). Also, I thank the publishers, Avery Color Studios of Marquette, Michigan, and

The IRVIN shares busy waters with an Interlake Steamship Company vessel (background) and a Coast Guard 180-foot buoy tender (middle) during the early 1950s. The billboard lettering distinctly identifies the IRVIN's owners. (Canal Park Marine Museum collection)

its staff for their services. I also owe many thanks to Glenn Blaszkiewicz, operations manager for the IRVIN, who has provided assistance throughout the project. He has offered his office space for my use, provided numerous useful comments after reviewing the manuscript, and, having worked with me on the IRVIN since its 1986 opening, has been able to check the accuracy of my information and remind me of important things I may have forgotten.

While I've learned a lot about the IRVIN since I started working on the boat, I have greatly expanded my knowledge over the past year thanks to the many people who assisted me in research. I especially thank C. Patrick Labadie, Thom

Holden, Kevin Gange, and Beth Duncan, the fine staff of the Canal Park Marine Museum in Duluth, for their assistance throughout this project. I have known these four for many years, and they have generously supplied me access to the Museum's files, photographs, and other artifacts in their collection pertaining to the IRVIN. Much of the IRVIN's cargo history at the end of the book was obtained due to their help. I also thank Peggy Bechtol of the Great Lakes Historical Society, Vermilion, Ohio, for supplying me with news clippings pertaining to events throughout the IRVIN's career; Stanley Jasek, Area Engineer with the U.S. Army Corps of Engineers at Sault Ste. Marie, Michigan; Trish Gingras of Skillings Mining Review; Tom Kucinski, IRVIN Volunteer, former Mate with USS Great Lakes Fleet, and general foreman with Duluth Missabe and Iron Range Railway in Two Harbors, Minnesota; and the staff of USS Great Lakes Fleet, the IRVIN's former owner, also deserve thanks for directing me to possible sources of information for the IRVIN's cargo history. A special thanks goes to Mark Barnes, Assistant Archivist with the Institute for Great Lakes Research in Perrysburg, Ohio, for his assistance on several aspects of the project. He has supplied me news clippings, given me access to photographs in the Institute's collection, and provided the final pieces of the puzzle regarding the IRVIN's cargo history. I have contacted him periodically throughout the past year with many questions, and I appreciate his helpful, timely response in each case.

When I completed the first draft of the manuscript, I asked several people to review the manuscript before I made any changes. It is nearly impossible to do an objective review of your own work and get meaningful results from it. These

reviewers all made a unique contribution, and their sugges-
tions are frequently incorporated in the final product. I thank
Glenn Blaszkiewicz; C. Patrick Labadie; Thom Holden; Darcy
(Pearson) Freese, IRVIN Tour Guide and Director from 1986
through 1990; Kent Lundahl, IRVIN Tour Guide since 1986;
Cedric Woodard, IRVIN Tour Guide since 1988, long time
Great Lakes sailor, and, for a few weeks my shipmate when I
sailed aboard the CASON J. CALLAWAY; Tom Holecek, IRVIN
Tour Guide since 1993; and Peter Westerman, IRVIN Tour
Guide in 1994. I selected each of these individuals because I
knew that all have an intense interest in the IRVIN and Great
Lakes ships in general, but also because I knew each would
offer a unique perspective to the manuscript and be able to
offer something different from the others.

Researching written documents, as helpful as they may
be, does not provide a complete picture of the history of the
IRVIN. I have had the opportunity to interview many people
associated with the vessel who provided me with insight I
could not have found elsewhere. I wish to thank Barb Stanley,
granddaughter of William A. Irvin, and her son, Scott, who
gave me a personal view of William A. Irvin's life, and Herb
"Sandy" White, grandson of William A. Irvin, who expanded
on the Stanley's information, especially concerning Irvin's
industrial career. I also wish to thank Chuck and Cleo Zalk,
who had the privilege to take a trip on the IRVIN as guests in
1969, for recalling their fond memories and for allowing me to
publish photographs taken of them during the trip. I also con-
ducted brief interviews with former IRVIN crewmembers who
came aboard for tours during 1994. Each of the following crewmen offered a different look at life on the boat, and I appreciate

them taking time out of their visits aboard to talk with me. I owe thanks to Byron DeZurik, Morris Hickok, Lee Permenter, Herbert Thorson, James Varner, and Patrick Kennedy for sharing their experiences aboard the boat. I also thank Bob Hom, Director of Operations for the Duluth Entertainment Convention Center, for his information regarding the DECC's acquisition of the IRVIN. I also thank Darcy Freese, Kent Lundahl, and Cedric Woodard for taking time to reminisce about the experiences we've shared aboard the IRVIN since it opened for tours.

Finally, I'd like to thank the entire 1994 IRVIN staff for their support during the project. They introduced me to many of the people I interviewed and filled in for me without hesitation when I took time out of the workday to conduct interviews or to scrounge through the boat in search of items to use for research. If I left anyone out of this list, it is accidental; I do not intend to slight anyone of the credit deserved for help on the project.

Jody Aho
Duluth, Minnesota
April 27, 1995

The IRVIN, downbound in the Detroit River in 1954. (Institute for Great Lakes Research collection)

William A. Irvin Fact Summary

Built: . . . . American Ship Building Co., Lorain, Ohio
Hull#: 811
Keel Laid: . . . . June 21, 1937
Launched: . . . . November 10, 1937
Sailed on maiden voyage: . . . . June 25, 1938
Keel Length: . . . . 586'0"
Overall Length: . . . . 610'9"
Width: . . . . 60'0"
Depth: . . . . 32'6"
Hatches: 18
Holds: 3
Capacity: . . . . 14,000 tons
Engines: . . . . Steam turbine
Horsepower: 2000
Boilers: . . . . Two coal-fired water tube boilers
Speed: . . . . . 11.1 Statute MPH loaded, 12.5 statute MPH light

Introduction

Shipping on the Great Lakes was created by the need to bring together two vast areas of raw materials in the Great Lakes region—rich iron ore fields and limestone deposits surrounding the upper Great Lakes and coal fields in Ohio, Pennsylvania, Kentucky, and West Virginia. These raw materials could be used to make steel and, subsequently, a wide variety of products which have become commonplace to the people of the United States, Canada, and the world. In the early- and mid-1800s, the United States was beginning its westward expansion. Along the shores of Lake Erie and southern Lake Michigan, there was an abundance of labor, and soon the nation's industrial Midwest was born. This location also made strategic use of its proximity to the Great Lakes, especially once a cost-effective way was developed to ship raw materials over its waters.

Iron ore was first discovered in the Great Lakes region in the 1840s near Marquette, Michigan, in Michigan's central Upper Peninsula. Since Lake Superior was nearby, it provided a convenient means to transport the iron ore to hungry markets to the south and east. In 1852, the first iron ore was shipped across the Great Lakes from the Marquette Iron Range to Pennsylvania. There was one major obstacle along this route which needed to be overcome if iron ore shipping was to grow.

On the St. Mary's River, at Sault Ste. Marie, there was a briskly flowing stretch of rapids, since there is a 21-foot drop between the upper (Lake Superior level) river and the lower (Lake Huron level) river. For years, cargoes were portaged through downtown Sault Ste. Marie (along the route of the city's present-day Portage Avenue) and re-loaded down river. In 1855, the State of Michigan constructed a lock to by-pass the rapids. The U.S. Army Corps of Engineers later took over operation and development of the lock, and today they operate four locks at Sault Ste. Marie.

Once a successful lock system was operating, larger ships could be constructed to handle the iron ore movement. In 1869, the R.J. HACKETT was constructed as the prototype for all lakers for roughly the next 100 years. The HACKETT incorporated a design to allow maximum cargo carrying capacity and convenience location of shipboard equipment. The pilothouse was constructed at the forward end—especially helpful on the Great Lakes because of frequent docking, operation in rivers and harbors, and convenience in times of poor visibility. The engine room was located aft, and crew quarters were constructed on both ends. The midsection of the vessel was a large open space free of obstructions on deck to make loading and unloading as easy as possible. The HACKETT carried well under 1000 tons per trip—tiny by today's standards—but its innovations have influenced ship design since.

The HACKETT, as were all vessels at the time, was constructed of wood. A stronger, more durable, longer life material was needed in ship construction. Soon, composite hulls of iron and wood were being constructed, until finally, in the 1880s, the first steel vessels were built. Fittingly, at nearly the

The WILLIAM A. IRVIN, downbound in the Detroit River in 1956 under full load. The large flag sports the vessel's name. (Institute for Great Lakes Research collection)

same time, iron ore was discovered in northern Minnesota. The first iron ore was shipped at Two Harbors on July 31, 1884, from the Vermillion Iron Range, approximately 65 miles north-northwest of Two Harbors. In 1890, the vast Mesabi Iron Range was discovered about 60 miles north of Duluth. Never before had iron ore of such high quality and in such great quantity been found. Duluth, which until that time was a slow growing port city which primarily handled grain, soon became known as a major iron ore shipping port. The Cuyuna Iron Range, about 80 miles west of Duluth, was also discovered, and its iron ore was shipped through Duluth's twin port in Superior, Wisconsin. With these major discoveries, the size of vessels on the Great Lakes grew quickly. A 300-footer was considered large in 1885; just ten years later, the 400-foot barrier was broken with construction of the VICTORY (which would sail the

Lakes until 1970). It took only five more years for shipbuilders to approach the 500-foot mark. The JAMES J. HILL, ISAAC L. ELLWOOD, WILLIAM EDENBORN, and JOHN W. GATES were each 497 feet long (but considered the first "500-footers") and were capable of carrying in excess of 8000 tons per trip. All four entered service in 1900. Great Lakes ships certainly experienced a huge transformation in size in just 31 years!

Until 1900, many Great Lakes ships were owned by sole proprietors. In many cases, that owner owned just the one vessel. There were few who owned large fleets of ships, and all operators of one-ship fleets were flirting with the danger of something happening to put their one ship out of service—a fire, collision, or shipwreck. Many small operators went out of business after they lost their only ship due to some unfortunate situation—and consequently lost their only means of making their deliveries. Not all operators had this worry, however, and five of the larger fleets in 1900 were the American Steamship Company (not to be confused with the Great Lakes fleet of the same name today, which was formed in 1907), the Bessemer Steamship Company, the Minnesota Steamship Company, the Mutual Steamship Company, and the National Steamship Company. The following spring these five fleets would be involved in the largest sale of vessels in Great Lakes history. The United States Steel Corporation was formed in 1901, and these five fleets were merged into one giant, 114-vessel fleet known as the Pittsburgh Steamship Company. No other fleet in Great Lakes history would ever come close to matching this size. Not only did the Pittsburgh Steamship Company become the largest fleet in terms of number of vessels, it also included the JAMES J. HILL class as well as many other large, new ore carriers, all dedicated to moving iron ore from Duluth, Superior, and Two Harbors down to new mills on the Lower Lakes.

With the support of U.S. Steel, the Pittsburgh Steamship Company set many trends itself and soon adopted the innovations incorporated in new vessels ordered by other fleets. In 1905, the fleet added four new vessels—the ELBERT H. GARY, the WILLIAM E. COREY, the GEORGE W. PERKINS, and the HENRY C. FRICK, which became the largest on the Great Lakes at the time. All were 569 feet long and were capable of carrying over 11,000 tons in one load. Even though all outlived their usefulness to U.S. Steel by the early 1960's, all found new homes in other fleets. The PERKINS was finally retired at the end of 1981 as the H.C. HEIMBECKER. In 1906, these four lost the honor of largest on the Lakes to a new class of vessel.

The 600-foot mark was reached for the first time in 1906 with construction of the DANIEL J. MORRELL and the EDWARD Y. TOWNSEND. While this pair of vessels spent their lives hauling ore mainly for Bethlehem Steel, U.S. Steel was not to be outdone. They added several 600-footers of their own in 1906 and, perhaps more significantly, used the plans of their first 600-footers as a standard for all vessels they would construct until 1930. Using an "off-the-shelf" plan cut building costs considerably, allowing U.S. Steel to build a large fleet of similar, large-sized vessels.

In 1929, the Great Lakes fleets, including Pittsburgh Steamship Company, were enjoying one of their best years ever. In addition to strong iron ore shipments, coal and limestone shipments—the other two ingredients needed in the steel-making recipe—were also robust. Grain shipping was also busy. Pittsburgh Steamship Company continued to add new boats to their fleet, and orders were placed for two new vessels in 1930. The fleet had dropped in size since its creation, as one new 600-footer would do the work of three 1890s vessels, but it still had over 70 vessels in 1929. The optimism all the fleets had was completely gone by the end of 1929. The United States was entering the Great Depression, and consumer confidence disappeared practically overnight. U.S. Steel's two vessels under construction at the time, the THOMAS W. LAMONT and the EUGENE P. THOMAS, were completed in 1930, only to find shipping lanes much quieter than they were just one year before. Any future ship construction was out of the question as the Depression deepened; in fact, many small, older vessels sailed their last.

Building the IRVIN and Restoring Confidence

S omething was needed to restore confidence in Great Lakes ship owners. The deepening Great Depression saw a tremendous drop in iron ore shipments. By 1932, less than four million tons of iron ore were being shipped on the Great Lakes, compared with more than 15 times that amount only three years earlier. Many boats remained laid up during the Great Depression; those that did sail fitted out for only a few trips and promptly returned to lay-up. No Great Lakes fleets saw the need to increase their carrying capacity by building new vessels.

By 1937, the nation's economy began to turn around. That spring, the Pittsburgh Steamship Company announced contracts for the construction of four new ore boats. The Great Lakes Engineering Works of River Rouge, Michigan, received orders for Hulls 285 and 286, the RALPH H. WATSON and the JOHN HULST. The other two boats would be built by the American Ship Building Company of Lorain, Ohio, as that yard's Hulls 810 and 811. Hull 810 became known as the GOVERNOR MILLER, named after New York governor Nathan Miller. Hull 811 became the WILLIAM A. IRVIN.

These new vessels were designed for several purposes. First, United States Steel wanted to express their confidence that the nearly eight-year economic downturn was over, and better times were at hand. Second, the vessels were designed to act as public relations tools for U.S. Steel, especially the GOVERNOR MILLER and the WILLIAM A. IRVIN. These two would feature an extra deck just for guests and a private dining room. Finally, the four boats included many of the latest technological advances and other features to improve the safety and comfort of those aboard.

During the spring of 1937, steel plates, beams, and rivets began to fill the shipyard at Lorain. Workers prepared building sites for both vessels. On June 21, the 586- foot long keel, a steel beam from which the remaining structure of the vessel would

This early photo of the IRVIN, taken in the shipyard in late June, 1937, shows the beginnings of the vessel. Less than five months later, the vessel would be launched. (*Rudy Moc Studio photo, DECC collection*)

The IRVIN gets her first taste of water on November 10, 1937. (Canal Park Marine Museum collection)

be built, was laid. The shipyard hired the Rudy Moc Studio of Lorain to take week-by-week photos of the IRVIN's construction progress, and shipyard officials prepared a weekly summary of the number of rivets used, the number of feet of welding, and the quantity of steel used to-date. By the end of August, the bottom, many of the side plates, the sides of the cargo holds, and part of the spar deck were assembled. On August 30, the stem of the vessel—the forward-most steel beam running perpendicular to the water line—was completed. Meanwhile, hatch covers were being pre-fabricated in another part of the yard, and all of them were completed by the end of September. A few weeks later, the spar deck was completed, and launching was near. The IRVIN was ready for its first taste of water, just one hundred and forty-two days after the keel was laid, on November 10, 1937. The IRVIN was far from being ready to sail—there was no smokestack, the after-cabins were nowhere near completion, much of the equipment had not been installed, and the forward end cabins were just a skeleton. Nonetheless, William A. Irvin and his wife, Gertrude, were on a train for Lorain to attend the launching, accompanied by industry officials. Others attending the launch included Benjamin F. Fairless, another top U.S. Steel executive (and who would become namesake of a new ore boat in 1942); Captain J.N. Rolfson of Wyandotte, Michigan, who would serve as the IRVIN's first skipper; William P. Bourlier of Fairhaven, Michigan, who would become the IRVIN's first chief engineer; and Spencer J. Kidd, who, unsuspected at the time, would become the IRVIN's Captain in 1967. Gertrude Irvin smashed the traditional bottle of champagne against the hull, and the IRVIN made its way down the timber launchways and into the adjacent slip. The IRVIN became the first of Pittsburgh Steamship Company's four new boats to be launched—the first new ore boat built on the Great Lakes in over seven years.

The IRVIN and the other three vessels were to become the largest vessels in the Pittsburgh Steamship Company fleet, with a capacity of just over 14,000 tons of iron ore at mid-summer draft. The vessels were only a few feet longer and six inches deeper than the fleet's largest to that time, and they were among the top 20 boats (when ranked by overall dimensions) on the Lakes in 1937. The 638-foot CARL D. BRADLEY, owned by the Michigan Limestone Corporation (U.S. Steel's limestone-carrying subsidiary) became the largest Great Lakes boat when it entered service July 27, 1927, and held that honor until

June of 1942. (However, the BRADLEY was engaged mainly in the limestone trade.) Among iron ore carriers, the 633-foot Canadian vessel LEMOYNE, owned by Canada Steamship Lines, and the 631-foot HARRY COULBY, owned by Cleveland-based Interlake Steamship Company, were the largest vessels regularly engaged in the iron ore trade. Thus, the IRVIN and its three sisters were not destined to set any records for the largest cargo carried, but they were expected to be productive members of the Great Lakes' largest fleet.

Over the winter of 1937-38, American Ship Building Company continued work on the IRVIN. The smokestack was added to the vessel early in 1938, and throughout the winter months, the cabins on both ends and the guest dining room were being furnished. By April 1, 1938, the statistics pertaining to the IRVIN's construction had reached impressive totals: 687,412 rivets driven; 103,453 feet (just over 19.5 miles) of welding completed; and over 4900 long tons of steel had been used.

After sea trials and subsequent adjustments were completed, the IRVIN was ready to sail on its first voyage. Although it was the first of the four new boats launched, it was the third one ready to sail. The first of the Great Lakes Engineering Works hulls, the JOHN HULST, was the first one to sail, beginning her maiden voyage on May 21, 1938. The GOVERNOR MILLER, the IRVIN's twin and shipyard mate, left Lorain on June 8 for her first load. The RALPH H. WATSON was still under construction at River Rouge; it would not sail until September 2.

On Saturday morning, June 25, Captain J.N. Rolfson guided the IRVIN through the highway drawbridge crossing the Black River in Lorain, through the piers, and out onto shal-

The Duluth Missabe & Iron Range Railway's ore docks in West Duluth loaded the IRVIN's first cargo on June 28, 1938. The IRVIN visited these docks 670 more times during its career. (Author's photo)

low Lake Erie on its first trip. The IRVIN made excellent time as it steamed up the Detroit River, across Lake St. Clair, past the many homes lining the St. Clair River shores, and up Lake Huron to Detour Reef Light, marking the entrance to the St. Mary's River. Just before sunset on Sunday, June 26, the IRVIN passed upbound through the Soo Locks and made her way through the upper St. Mary's River, Whitefish Bay, and onto Lake Superior. At 2:15 a.m. on Tuesday, June 28, the IRVIN passed underneath Duluth's Aerial Lift Bridge and progressed through the harbor to the Duluth Missabe & Iron Range Railway docks for its first load of iron ore. Six hours and thirty-five minutes later, the IRVIN made its way underneath the Aerial Bridge again, this time with her first load of iron ore, bound for the National Tube Company dock in Lorain, Ohio.

William A. Irvin

*"He was a giant of a man, physically
and socially. He was very powerful."*

–Barbara Stanley,
William A. Irvin's granddaughter

The IRVIN's namesake became the fourth president of U.S. Steel and chairman of the board based completely on self-taught experience in the work world. William A. Irvin was born to contractor David S. Irvin and Sophia Bergman Irvin on December 7, 1873, in Indiana, Pennsylvania (about 50 miles east of Pittsburgh). The elder Irvin died at a young age, and with a younger brother and mother to help support, William dropped out of school at the end of 8th grade. He became a telegraph operator for the Pennsylvania Railroad (now part of the large ConRail system which covers the northeastern U.S. and, coincidentally, hauls some of the iron ore from Lake Erie unloading docks to steel mills farther inland). Later William moved up to become a shipping and freight clerk for the railroad.

Before he was 20, William married Luella May Cunningham, the daughter of one of the wealthiest families in Indiana, Pennsylvania. William and Luella had five children in the space of nine years: Martha, Mildred, Louise, William

William A. Irvin's five children are taking a summer vacation aboard their father's namesake during the mid-1940s. Left to right: Arch, Mildred, Alice, Martha, Louise. (Duluth Entertainment Convention Center collection, courtesy of Barb Stanley)

Archibald (commonly referred to as "Arch"), and Alice. (The children died in reverse order of birth; Alice died relatively young, while Martha survived to age 92.)

William entered the steel industry in 1895 as a shipping clerk with the Apollo Steel Company of Apollo, Pennsylvania. He moved up through the ranks quickly, and by 1904, he became the assistant to the vice president of the American Sheet and Tin Plate Company after it absorbed Apollo. Unfortunately, Luella passed away during childbirth at an early age, before any of the five children were through school. Not long afterwards, at a business meeting in Denver, William

The Irvin family on board for a trip during the mid-1940s. Front row, left to right: Martha, William, Gertrude, and Louise. Back row, left to right: Arch, Mildred, Alice. (Duluth Entertainment Convention Center collection, courtesy of Barb Stanley)

met an attractive red-haired woman named Emma Gertrude Gifford.

She (who commonly used Gertrude) was born on May 1, 1881 (conflicting data shows Iowa and St. Paul, Minnesota, as places of birth). She moved to the Denver area and, in 1910, married William A. Irvin. Relatives remember her as a gorgeous woman with an interesting personality. "She taught me how to rumba," recalls Barbara Stanley, granddaughter of William A. Irvin. But Gertrude was certainly not all play and no work. She and William both expected things to be done the way they wanted them to be done.

William and Gertrude Irvin relax on the deck behind the captain's office during one of their many trips aboard the vessel. This view dates from the mid-1940s. (Duluth Entertainment Convention Center *collection, courtesy of Barb Stanley)*

"It was not beneath her at all, with a house full of servants, to wash windows," remembers Stanley. "If she didn't like something, she did it herself."

"She, more than anyone else, guided his career," commented Herb "Sandy" White, grandson of William A. Irvin.

William continued to advance upward through the American Sheet and Tin Plate Company. He moved to New York City for the company, and returned to Pittsburgh around the start of World War I. In 1924, he became vice president of operations, a position he held for seven years. In 1931, he and Gertrude moved back to New York City, where William joined the United States Steel Corporation. A year later, William

Amelia Irvin (William's daughter-in-law), William A. Irvin, and his daughter Louise were on board for a trip in this mid-1940s photo.
(Duluth Entertainment Convention Center collection, courtesy of Barb Stanley)

became U.S. Steel's president. He guided the nation's largest steelmaker through the depressed 1930s economy and, in 1938, became vice chairman of the board for United States Steel Corporation.

The same year, his namesake freighter began hauling loads of iron ore from northeastern Minnesota's many iron ore mines to the blast furnaces on the lower lakes. William and Gertrude were the first guests aboard the new freighter, and took several trips aboard in the subsequent years, with industrialists of the day. The Irvin children and grandchildren were given a different perspective on the key public figures that they wouldn't have received otherwise.

"He had a large sphere of friends," states Barbara Stanley. "He knew Eisenhower before he (Eisenhower) became President (of the United States). We grandkids appreciated people, things, and places we wouldn't have otherwise. They (William and Gertrude) owned a beautiful island in Canada, and we summered there."

"He was a disciplinarian with his kids, grandkids, and his associates with the steel company," Herb White recalls. "Hard work was one of his tenets, and he proved it by going to work when he was twelve years old."

For Herb, these summer outings were his way to get to know his grandfather. "Most of my growing-up years, he was in New York. During those two-week vacations, we really got to know him." In addition to his work in steel, William showed great concern for industrial safety. He was injured in one of his earlier jobs, and this led to a lifelong push for safer work methods. This concern included the WILLIAM A. IRVIN and its sister ships, which were "a triumph of safety, comfort, and capacity," according to William's remarks at his namesake's launching. He became active in the National Safety Council, and became its chairman of the board in 1942. Herb White remembers his grandfather as "a pioneer in industrial safety." Appropriately, the WILLIAM A. IRVIN had a relatively accident-free 40-year career, thanks to the vessel's safety features and U.S. Steel's strong emphasis on safety.

In the early 1950s, William was nearing the end of his eighth decade of life. Late in 1951, he was admitted to the Harkness Pavilion of the Columbia-Presbyterian Medical Center in New York. After a long illness, William died on January 1, 1952, at age 78. He is buried in the Homewood

Cemetery in Pittsburgh. Gertrude died in New York City on June 7, 1956, at the age of 75. Many of William A. Irvin's grandchildren are still alive (in various parts of the United States), and they, along with their children, still have fond memories of the man Barbara Stanley described as "the last of the self-taught giants."

Gertrude Irvin smashes the traditional bottle of champagne against the hull before the IRVIN made its way down the timber launchways on November 10, 1937. (Duluth Entertainment Convention Center collection)

The IRVIN's Technological Innovations

"They were pretty well automated for that time. It was pretty remarkable."

–Patrick N. Kennedy, IRVIN coalpasser and fireman in 1941-42, recalling the IRVIN's advances in technology

While William A. Irvin, at his namesake's launching, highlighted the safety features of the new boat, he did not emphasize the many technical advances (although they contribute to the boat's safety). They, too, could be considered a triumph at the time. Many of the advances were found in the engine room, but there were several features added in other parts of the boat as well.

The IRVIN and its sister ships were the first bulk freighters on the Great Lakes to use steam turbine engines with reduction gear to drive the propeller shaft. Prior to this, most ore boats on the Great Lakes were equipped with reciprocating steam engines. Most reciprocating engines were triple expansion engines, meaning they had three cylinders. Each cylinder would be a different size to correspond with a gradual loss in steam pressure. The high pressure cylinder would average 24 inches in diameter and would receive the steam coming out of

The IRVIN's propeller is more than 15 feet in diameter. (Duluth Entertainment Convention Center collection)

the boilers. After passing through the high pressure cylinder, the steam passes through the intermediate cylinder, about 40 inches in diameter. The lower pressure steam would then push on one last cylinder, a large one which could range up to 72 inches across, before exhausting to the condenser. The machinery for such an engine would easily fill a two- to three-story engine room, yet produce just over 2200 horsepower (or even less for smaller engines). Some vessels used a quadruple expansion reciprocating engine, which worked off the same principle as the triple expansion except for an additional intermediate-pressure cylinder. In 1924, the Ford Motor Company

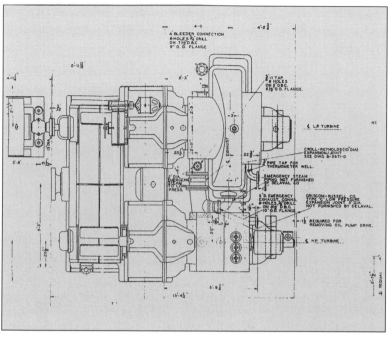

Diagram of engines and reduction gear. (Instruction Manual, DeLaval Steam Turbine Co.)

decided to try a different type of engine on two new ore boats the company had ordered. The BENSON FORD and the HENRY FORD II became the Lakes' first diesel-powered boats when they entered service early in August, 1924. The following year, the Michigan Limestone Corporation self-unloader T.W. ROBINSON became the first turbo-electric vessel on the Great Lakes. Boilers produced steam to power turbines, which in turn ran electrical generators for a motor to turn the shaft and propeller. Relatively few vessels with turbo-electric engines ever entered service on the Lakes, and diesel would not become popular for many years. Continuing its trend of setting

The CANADIAN LEADER was the last vessel built on the Great Lakes with a steam turbine engine, marking the end of an era started by the IRVIN and its sister ships. The CANADIAN LEADER is shown here inbound Duluth piers on April 8, 1995. (Author's photo)

other "firsts" on the Great Lakes, Pittsburgh Steamship Company decided to install the DeLaval-built, cross-compound, double-reduction-geared turbines on board its four newest vessels, with a direct drive to the propeller through reduction gear (no electric motors to run the propeller). Many engineers consider the turbine to be the most maintenance-free engine for shipboard use; many diesel-powered boats, by comparison, have had numerous breakdowns after only a few years of service. However, the turbine has one major disadvantage for use on the Great Lakes—it cannot change speeds quickly. A turbine can reach close to full speed right away, but it takes up to a few hours to get the last few revolutions on the propeller. The same situation is true when coming into port or a river from the open lake. The turbine cannot be slowed down quickly, either, without blowing the safety valves. Coming into Duluth Harbor, for instance, turbine-powered vessels often begin slowing down while still several miles out in the lake and continue to do so all the way through the harbor. While diesel-powered boats also reduce speed before entering confined water, they are able to do so faster. Despite these drawbacks, the turbine was the engine of choice on new boats for nearly 30 years. The CANADIAN LEADER, the last new turbine-powered boat on the Great Lakes, entered service October 12, 1967. As diesels became relatively inexpensive compared to turbines, they began their surge in popularity in the early 1960s and were used exclusively in new vessels after 1967.

The turbines produced 2000 horsepower, slightly less than the standard 2200 horsepower triple-expansion engines

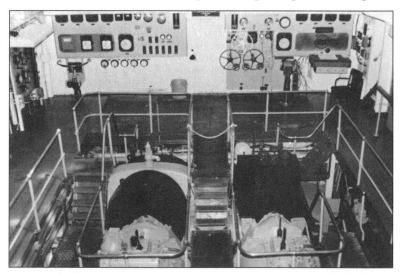

The IRVIN's 2000 HP steam turbines, among the first of their type on the Great Lakes. *(Canal Park Marine Museum collection)*

The IRVIN's pilothouse, showing the electric (left) and telemotor (right) steering wheels. *(Canal Park Marine Museum collection)*

used on new Pittsburgh Steamship Company vessels from 1916 through 1930. They would turn the propeller shaft at an average speed of between 83 and 86 RPM, but 90 RPM could be maintained for short periods. Ironically, the slightly lower horsepower meant the IRVIN could travel only 11.1 statute miles per hour loaded, compared with around 11.5 MPH for most other vessels in the fleet with the higher horsepower engines. This difference, while small, added up during a round trip. Most other vessels in the fleet could complete a round trip in around six-and-a-half days. The IRVIN rarely made a round trip in under seven days and, according to a fleet record book from the 1960s, was the slowest vessel in the entire fleet.

The IRVIN's boiler room was among the first to feature an automatic coal-conveying system to carry the coal from the coal bunker to the fireboxes. At the fireboxes, the IRVIN was equipped with two Firite spreader-type stokers for each boiler. A stoker is a mechanical arm which pushes the coal into the firebox and spreads it around, thus eliminating the need for firemen and coalpassers to hand shovel coal into the fireboxes. The IRVIN became one of the more fuel efficient boats in the fleet, averaging around 2400 pounds per hour. Many boats at the time were burning between 3000 and 4000 pounds of coal per hour. Still, at least two men in the boiler room attended to other jobs, such as cleaning grates, emptying the ashes, and monitoring the water level in the boilers.

The IRVIN's steering gear system was also among the first of its type on the Great Lakes. Many older boats had steam steering engines which drove the rudder, and chains connected the steering wheel in the pilothouse to the steering gear. The IRVIN had a hydro electric steering system with two wheels in the pilothouse. The more commonly used wheel was electrically connected from the pilothouse to the steering gear and was easy to turn. As the wheelsman turned the wheel, valves electrically opened the proper way to allow hydraulic fluid to be pumped into a large piston connected to the rudder post. The other wheel, the telemotor, was the back-up system. There was a small oil pump in the base of the telemotor. When the telemotor wheel was turned, the pump pushed hydraulic fluid back through pipes to a connector on the steering gear. The connector then ran the steering gear motors. In combination with the electric wheel, there was a Sperry Gyro-Pilot. This was the vessel's automatic pilot for use on the open lake since the vessel often held the same course for hours at a time. The gyro-compass was connected to the steering gear and any time it sensed a slight change in course, the correct angle of rudder would be applied to bring the vessel back to the preset course. This eliminated having an exhausted wheelsman make continual variations in course, resulting in a noticeable snake-like wake behind the vessel (and wasted time and energy).

Structurally, the IRVIN included several innovations. The IRVIN and its sister ships were the first boats to include fully-enclosed tunnels running underneath the spar deck, one on each side. Before this, boats would have an open catwalk on top of the ballast tanks, but this would not be accessible if the vessel's holds were completely filled. While there were lifelines which ran from one end of the boat to the other, they would do nothing to keep a person from getting wet when a wave came across the deck. On the IRVIN that tunnel was completely enclosed (at the expense of having less cubic capacity in the holds for coal and limestone cargoes). The web frames, steel supports spaced 12 feet apart throughout the sides with human-sized openings cut in them, made for constant bumping and tripping hazards as a crewman traversed the tunnel, but it was much safer in heavy weather than being out on the open deck.

The spar deck itself consisted of 18 hatches on 24-foot centers, meaning there was 24 feet from the center of one hatch to the center of the next hatch. Sixteen of these were of the then new one-piece type with an electric hatch crane to remove and replace them. This system was first introduced to the Lakes in 1925. The first two hatches were the old telescoping type, a necessity because the guest dining room was in the way of the hatch crane on deck. Finally, the entrances to the after-end crew's quarters were through interior hallways, not individual doors opening to the outside of the vessel. With the fully enclosed tunnels, a crewmember was able to go from his or her room to most other parts of the boat without going on deck.

The IRVIN is one of the few Great lakes vessels to be retired while still holding a Great Lakes cargo record. On August 27, 1940, the IRVIN set the Great Lakes record for the fastest unloading of an iron ore cargo using shoreside equipment. The IRVIN unloaded 13,856 gross tons of iron ore in 2 hours, 55 minutes (including the time taken to arrive and depart the dock) in Conneaut, Ohio. This record still stands today, and the IRVIN will likely continue to hold the record long into the future, since almost all iron ore is now handled by self-unloaders. (Canal Park Marine Museum collection)

Excerpt from IRVIN logbook, 1972, noting the bitterly cold conditions of the spring of 1972 on Lake Superior near Duluth. Ice is usually gone from Lake Superior by the end of April.

Life Aboard the Boat

"This was the greatest job I ever had in my life."

–Lee Permenter, a deckwatch on
the IRVIN in 1963

"They treated us like kings and queens."

–Chuck and Cleo Zalk, guests
on the IRVIN, July 12-19, 1969.

*L*ife aboard a Great Lakes ore boat is much different than life ashore. A crewmember leaves family behind on shore to live and work with thirty other people who become a sort of "family" themselves. He or she is confined to the vessel, with only a few hours ashore every couple of days, but it is hard to find privacy aboard the boat. Before companies started offering vacations during mid-season, a crewmember might leave home in late March and not return until after Christmas. The boat's schedule is unpredictable—fog, storms, or breakdowns may interrupt the vessel's schedule for days at a time. Many sailors have adapted to this unique lifestyle and have worked the boats for over 40 years. Many others have left the Lakes after only a few trips, not willing to make the sacrifices necessary for a life on the Lakes.

For meals for guests on the IRVIN, there was a private dining room with its own galley. At least two extra cooks hired for the summer months tended to all services needed by the guests while on board. (Canal Park Marine Museum collection)

A casual observer watching the boats from vantage points such as Duluth's Canal Park, the observation platforms at the Soo Locks, or from the shores of the St. Clair River, often desires to go aboard and travel to wherever the boat is going. Many steel, railroad, and automotive industry leaders, among others, took advantage of the opportunity to take a seven-day, all expenses paid round trip on the IRVIN, without having to commit to staying on for an entire season. Most boats on the Great Lakes have at least one spare room which is used for occasional guests, but the IRVIN had much more extensive and exquisite accommodations. Four walnut-paneled guest state-rooms could hold up to eight guests. A guest lounge, complete with a refrigerator, bar, and in later years, TV, provided room for card games and socializing (with a panoramic view through large windows). For meals, there was a private dining room with its own galley. At least two extra cooks hired for the summer months tended to all services needed by the guests while on board. On deck, there were additional activities. Guests frequently enjoyed drinks and snacks on a patio behind the upper deck of guest rooms, which included drink tables and lounge chairs, and on the spar deck between hatches 5 and 6, there was shuffleboard. Guests found their own way to pass the time as well, including kite-flying contests and walks around the deck (to burn off extra pounds gained from the ele-gant meals in the private dining room). Guests could even practice driving golf balls off the hatch covers! During the voy-age, the guests would make their way up to the pilothouse and down to the engine room to observe the vessel's crew at work. The IRVIN's dual function as iron ore carrier and public rela-tions tool provided a shipboard lifestyle both similar and dif-ferent from other ore boats.

The Image

The IRVIN's two roles were very distinct from a crewmember's standpoint. While the Captain and the Chief Engineer often interacted with the guests, other crewmembers were not to speak to the guests unless spoken to first. The brass rails throughout the boat were polished frequently, and the engine room was kept in immaculate condition. While guests were aboard, the crew, except for cleaning and housekeeping, was not allowed in the guest areas. Patrick Kennedy recalls how removed he and the rest of the boiler room crew were from the guests' activities.

"We just went about our business," Kennedy stated. "I've never been in the dining room. That would be unthinkable. We could be out on deck and if they walked by, we wouldn't say anything to them, and they wouldn't say anything to us."

A Guest Life

It's doubtful that, out of all the guests that sailed aboard the IRVIN, there were any who were disappointed by their stay (except, possibly, for a group of General Motors executives who took a trip in the early 1950s and had to get off after only four days because they were needed back at their office). Guests were satisfied with all aspects of their trips.

"We mostly drank and had fun," remembered Chuck and Cleo Zalk, two of the guests on board during the Gary-Two Harbors round trip from July 12-19, 1969. Chuck, owner of St. Paul-based Zalk Steel and Supply Company, was invited aboard by Ken Dorman, then St. Paul District Manager for U.S. Steel. The group wrote a long poem which described in detail their seven-day vacation. Many sets of guests on board decided to come up with a group name, and the Zalk group named themselves the "Minnesota Oredorables" since they all hailed from the Twin Cities area.

"We were eight people who got along really well," Cleo recalls. "It (some other groups) wasn't always a good mix."

The Zalks have many memories of their trip. The food on board was among the first things mentioned.

One facet of traveling as a guest aboard the WILLIAM A. IRVIN was enjoying elegant meals in the guest dining room. The eight guests shown here in these photos taken July 18, 1969, were about to have their final dinner aboard, hosted by the IRVIN's Captain and Chief Engineer. Shown are Chuck Zalk, President of Zalk Steel Company and his wife Cleo; John Maxon, President of Maxon Corporation and his wife Chris; Norm Lorentzen, Vice President of Northern Pacific Railway and his wife Helen; and Ken Dorman, regional Manager of Sales for U.S. Steel and his wife Helen. All eight were from the St. Paul area and nicknamed themselves the "Minnesota Oredorables."

(Spencer J. Kidd photo, Duluth Entertainment Convention Center collection)

"I remember fresh blueberries and raspberries," Cleo noted. "We had them for breakfast and then for dessert. The Captain and Chief Engineer joined us for dinner."

Chuck remembers the hospitality.

The lower port side guest stateroom, shortly after the IRVIN entered service. While the furnishings remained basically unchanged over the years, the room was redecorated several times. (DECC collection)

"In general, I remember the congeniality of the whole crew," Chuck said.

Guest logs were kept during most of the IRVIN's career, and each group of guests recorded its impressions of the trip. Captain Spencer J. Kidd, who commanded the IRVIN from 1967 through 1971, supplemented the guests' remarks with comments and pictures of his own. While some especially ambitious groups cut pictures out of magazines for collages, most groups wrote poems. As an example, John and Margaret Heizerling of Houston, Texas complimented the dining on board during their August 9-16, 1969, voyage:

"To David and Charles, our erstwhile cooks
Whose recipes can't be found in books
Our profound thanks for a job well done
The belts on our britches have expanded some."

The logs were used by many groups as a lasting way to say thanks to the captain of the vessel. Vivian and George Hayes, Jane and Don Selby, Kay and Frank Miller, and Margie and Bruce Matthews thanked Captain Kidd in a short poem after their June 26-July 3, 1971, trip:

"Hail, hail to our Captain Kidd
Safe to Duluth and back, he did
On Lake Michigan we are
Let's not go home—keep open the bar
We've never missed the office at all
We've never missed the kids—what a ball
So to Captain Kidd we say
Thank You For Our Great Stay!!!"

Crewmember Lives

Each crewmember who sails on the Great Lakes, whether forty years or forty days, has some experiences that they remember from their time on the boats. Each one gives a slightly different insight into life aboard the ore boats, and the crewmembers on the IRVIN were no exception. Many crewmembers enjoyed being on the vessel, even with the extra work required to maintain the IRVIN's special image. Byron DeZurik, an oiler on the IRVIN during part of the 1966 season, remembers the IRVIN as a boat where crewmen liked to keep their assignments aboard.

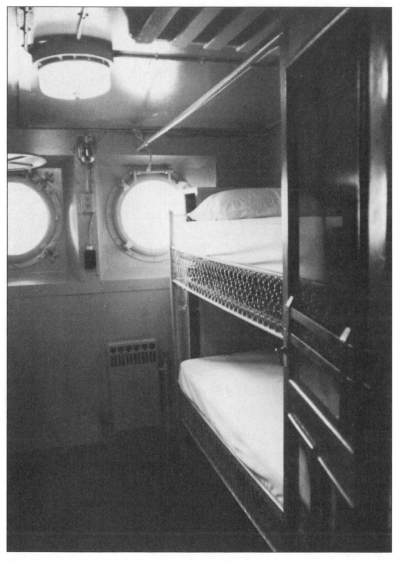

Despite many of the other advances the IRVIN made over other boats, the crew quarters remained rather spartan. (Duluth Entertainment Convention Center collection)

"Most of the crew was older; I was young," remembers DeZurik. "Everything was good on this ship, so they stayed with the ship."

Morris Hickok, a fireman on the IRVIN in 1965, reaped some of the benefits of sailing on a boat that carried guests. He quickly became friends with the guest cooks, and sampled some of the guest lifestyles in a different way.

"He (the guest cook) knew that I came from the East coast. Everyone else was from this area (Duluth and Two Harbors). He'd save leftover lobster for me."

Even if they didn't get leftover lobster, other crewmen still agreed that the IRVIN's food was the best they'd ever eaten. James Varner sailed on the IRVIN as a coalpasser in 1948 and recalls the food on board.

"We had the best cook," remembers Varner. "It was unquestionably the best food I've ever eaten."

Many crewmembers sailed only during the summer months when the weather was good and there were many chances to fill in for vacationing crewmen. Lee Permenter, a deckwatch on the IRVIN during the summer of 1963, enjoyed his time aboard for many reasons.

"This is the greatest job I ever had in my life. They were great guys to work with. We pulled vacation relief and a lot of guys like myself got a chance to make a lot of money."

Like all jobs, there were drawbacks, and not all crewmen enjoyed their time aboard. Herbert Thorson sailed on the IRVIN as a fireman from 1964 through 1966. His dad was a captain on the Great Lakes and got him the job. Thorson remembers the conditions in the boiler room.

"Hot, miserable. I never did like hot," Thorson said.

Work on the IRVIN continued during the winter. The pilothouse had been chipped and is ready for a new coat of paint as part of the ongoing maintenance work.   *(Duluth Entertainment Convention Center collection)*

Morris Hickok confirms the fact that sailing is a tough job for someone with a family life. "It's a nice job, but not a good job if you're married. You have to have complete trust (in your wife)," Hickok commented.

The boat's schedule can be very unpredictable. Before cellular phones, fax machines, and ship-to-shore phone hook-ups, boat's orders remained a mystery for most of a trip.

"We never knew where we were going (to load) until we got to the Soo," remembers James Varner.

Ice was another problem for the IRVIN, and many winters it caused trouble. Patrick Kennedy recalls one time the ice overpowered the IRVIN in 1941.

"We were on the Detroit River and got stuck in ice with our anchor down. The ice pushed us down the river 900 feet."

Herbert Thorson notes one time in 1965 when the ice was even more stubborn, and the IRVIN required outside help.

"We were stuck in ice, and the WOODRUSH (Coast Guard buoy tender and ice breaker) had to come and get us."

Crewmembers respected the IRVIN's captain, who was always selected from among the most experienced captains in the fleet. James Varner always showed his respect for the IRVIN's captain.

"The captain is someone that you really love. He really knows the Lakes."

Varner's respect must have paid off, especially in bad weather.

"I never got seasick in here," proclaimed Varner.

Form 1346.

Dock No. *E. 6*
Str. *IRVIN*
Grade *5z.*
Block *8/5*

Estimated weight in cargo _____ Tons
Number of Cars *190*

DULUTH, MISSABE AND IRON RANGE RAILWAY COMPANY

POCKET LIST

Pocket	Cars	Hatch	Pocket	Cars	Hatch	Pocket	Cars	Hatch	Pocket	Cars	Hatch	Pocket	Cars	Hatch
1			65			129			193			257	2	7	321	4	4
3			67			131			195			259	2	6	323	4	5
5			69			133			197			261	2	6	325	4	5
7			71			135			199			263	3	14	327	4	6
9			73			137			201			265	3	9	329	4	5
11			75			139			203	1		267	8		331	4	6
13			77			141			205	1		269	2	8	333	4	7
15			79			143			207	1		271	3	15	335	4	7
17			81			145			209	3		273	4	16	337	4	6
19			83			147			211	1		275	4	10	339	4	6
21			85			149			213			277	5	18	341	4	9
23			87			151			215	1		279	4	18	343	4	6
25			89			153			217	1		281	4	8	345	4	10
27			91			155			219	1		283	4	12	347	4	10
29			93			157			221	1		285	1	13	349	4	11
31			95			159			223	1		287	4	15	351	4	11
33			97			161			225	1		289			353	4	11
35			99			163			227	1		291	4	11	355	4	11
37			101			165			229	1		293		18	357	4	13
39			103			167			231	1		295	4	15	359	4	13
41			105			169			233	1		297	4	15	361	4	
43			107			171			235	1		299	4	16	363	4	11
45			109			173			237	2		301	4	13	365	4	15
47			111			175			239	1		303	4	13	367	4	16
49			113			177			241	SKIP		305	4	9	369	4	17
51			115			179			243	SKIP		307	4	8	371	4	16
53			117			181			245	2,6		309	1	7	373	4	15
55			119			183			247	4		311	4	8	375	4	16
57			121			185			249	3		313	2	9	377	4	17
59			123			187			251	4		315	4	2	379	4	16
61			125			189			253	4		317	4	3	381	4	
63			127			191			255	4	5	319	4	5	389	4	

The IRVIN's mates used pocket lists like this one to help them load iron ore. It lists how many cars of iron ore are in each pocket in the ore dock. This list is for a load out of D.M. & I.R.'s dock 6, east side, in Duluth.

The IRVIN's 40-Year Career

"To Our Skipper:

From Messabi Ridge (sic) to Blue Water Bridge
And down through the Strait of Belle Isle
We enjoyed every knot with that canny old Scot
Colin Campbell Carlisle."
–from the guest log written by Walter G.
Thomas, Marion P. Parsons, Lewis M. Parsons,
Ruth A. Shoop, and Duke Shoop, guests on the
IRVIN, September 21-28, 1950.

T he Blue Water Bridge and Detroit's Belle Isle were two of many landmarks the IRVIN passed frequently during her 40-year career on the Lakes. The loading port for the IRVIN's first cargo, Duluth, would become the most frequent port of call for the IRVIN, followed by nearby Two Harbors, just 26 miles up the shore from downtown Duluth. Each year, at least half of the boat's trips originated at those two ports, and many IRVIN crewmembers made their homes in that area. The IRVIN, as well as Pittsburgh Steamship Company's other vessels, regularly visited four ports with iron ore cargoes: South Chicago, Illinois; Gary, Indiana; Lorain, Ohio; and Conneaut, Ohio. The first three were homes to steel mills; Conneaut was a transfer port where iron ore was

The WILLIAM A. IRVIN is ready to begin taking on iron ore at the Duluth Missabe and Iron Range Railway docks, in Two Harbors in 1950. (Canal Park Marine Museum collection)

dropped off and reloaded onto trains run by the Bessemer and Lake Erie Railroad. The trains then delivered the iron ore to mills in the Pittsburgh area, 120 miles south of Conneaut. Some U.S. Steel vessels occasionally visited Cleveland, but not the IRVIN. Close to 90% of the IRVIN's trips were for loads of iron ore. Of the remaining cargoes, the majority was limestone. Most of the limestone was loaded at the Michigan Limestone Corporation dock in Calcite (Rogers City), Michigan, adjacent to the world's largest limestone quarry (60 miles southeast of the Mackinac Bridge). In 1956, the IRVIN began calling at the new limestone loading facility in Port Dolomite (Cedarville), Michigan, in the extreme eastern Upper Peninsula, on the northwestern Lake Huron shore. Most of the limestone was taken to Lower Lakes steel mills, but a few loads were taken to various docks in the Duluth-Superior area. The IRVIN didn't take on its first load of coal until 1957, and only carried the cargo sporadically over the next 21 years. Coal has usually been handled by self-unloading vessels, and with the tunnels running under the IRVIN's decks, the boat did not have good cubic capacity in its holds for the low-density cargo. The IRVIN also carried four loads of slag, a steel-making by-product, during its career. One slag cargo was carried during the 1938 season; the other three were carried toward the end of the IRVIN's

The changes in fleet markings are visible in this photo of the IRVIN, upbound in Lake St. Clair in July, 1958. The large "PITTSBURGH STEAMSHIP DIVISION" billboard lettering is gone, and the circular U.S. Steel logo has shrunk and moved to a location beneath the vessel's name. (Institute of Great Lakes Research collection)

career. All four slag cargoes originated at U.S. Steel's docks in Buffington, Indiana (not far from the Gary Works) and South Chicago, and all were taken to Duluth. Other unusual loading places for the IRVIN included four loads of iron ore out of Ashland, Wisconsin (70 miles east of Duluth), two loads of iron ore out of the Great Northern Railway (now Burlington Northern Santa Fe) ore docks in Superior, and a stone load out of Drummond Island, Michigan.

The IRVIN remained basically unchanged during its first ten years. With new improvements to the lake vessels after World War II, the IRVIN received an important addition at the start of the 1948 season—its first radar set. While a few lake vessels carried experimental sets earlier in the 1940s, radar did not come into widespread use until after World War II. Radar would become priceless during periods of low visibility, and it would provide navigational assistance. In 1950, an exterior change was made to the IRVIN. The fleet added the words "PITTSBURGH STEAMSHIP COMPANY" and the circular U.S. Steel logo to the sides of their boats, as was the practice of many Great Lakes fleets. Three years later, the Pittsburgh Steamship Company became known as the Pittsburgh Steamship Division of the United States Steel Corporation, and the side billboard reflected the change. Later in the 1950s, the billboard was dropped, and only a small U.S. Steel logo appeared under the name at the bow. The U.S. Steel logo was added to the black portion of the stack at this time. Besides the slight changes in the IRVIN's paint scheme mentioned earlier, there was one other time the IRVIN took on a slightly different appearance. The IRVIN and its fleetmates carried a special Bicentennial paint scheme during the 1976 season, including

The IRVIN is decorated for the nation's Bicentennial in 1976 in this view at Halett #5 in West Duluth. (Canal Park Marine Museum collection)

red and blue stars around the forward cabins. The fleet's name was officially changed again in 1964 to United States Steel Corporation Great Lakes Fleet, and three years later, both the former Pittsburgh Steamship Company boats (used mainly on the runs to Duluth and Two Harbors) and the Michigan Limestone Corporation boats (the "Bradley Fleet," used mainly to haul limestone), were merged together as one fleet. Even today, U.S. Steel's iron ore carriers and the former Bradley Fleet boats often continue separate roles, and the crews are still often assigned with geographical preferences in mind. The predominantly iron ore haulers have many crewmen from Northern

Minnesota and cities near the Lower lake unloading ports, while the limestone haulers have many crewmen from the Rogers City, Michigan, area.

While all Great Lakes vessels experience some stormy weather each year, shipwrecks are fewer and farther between, especially in recent years. Since 1938, there have been only a handful of storms on the Lakes which resulted in shipwrecks. The IRVIN laid up for the season about three weeks before the November 10, 1975 sinking of the EDMUND FITZGERALD in eastern Lake Superior. On November 29, 1966, the IRVIN was laid up as the DANIEL J. MORRELL broke in two north of Harbor Beach in Lake Huron. In 1958, the IRVIN was already laid up on November 18, as the once-largest vessel on the Lakes, the CARL D. BRADLEY, suddenly broke apart and sank in northern Lake Michigan. The IRVIN was on the Lower Lakes on the morning of May 11, 1953, as water flooded in through the hatches of the 440-foot HENRY STEINBRENNER off Isle Royale on Lake Superior, sinking her. But, the IRVIN did not escape the Armistice Day Storm of 1940.

The storm blew ashore on November 7 in Washington State, collapsing the Tacoma-Narrows suspension bridge. Ahead of the storm, the northern Great Plains were experiencing mild Indian summer-like weather. Many duck hunters were fooled by the mild weather—they went out without any cold-weather gear—and many froze to death as the storm and trailing cold front swept eastward on November 10. From a meteorological viewpoint, this storm was the worst to have ever hit the Great Lakes. It brought with it high winds, extremely low barometric pressures, and sudden temperature drops as it raced along. In Duluth, barometric pressure fell to

The WILLIAM A. IRVIN departing the Soo Locks downbound with a cargo of iron ore in the summer of 1940. Later that year, the vessel would wrestle with one of the Great Lakes' most severe storms ever. (Institute for Great Lakes Research collection)

28.66" (a city record which stood until January 10, 1975). Snow clogged most streets and roads throughout Minnesota.

On Lake Michigan, November 10, 1940, was still a quiet, mild fall day. Late in the day, the 440-foot WILLIAM B. DAVOCK, owned by the Interlake Steamship Company, and the 400-foot Canadian bulk freighter ANNA C. MINCH passed through the Straits of Mackinac and headed south on Lake Michigan. The morning of November 11 found an eerie-looking sky over the center of the lake as the two vessels continued toward their destinations. Up on Lake Superior, the IRVIN was downbound with a load of iron ore, loaded the previous day in Two Harbors.

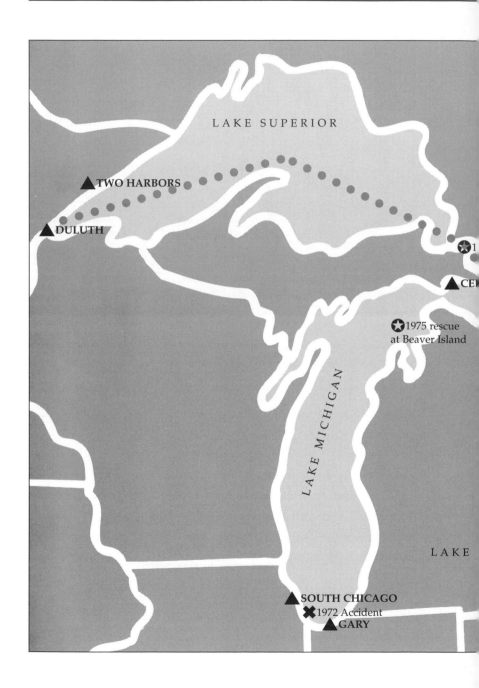

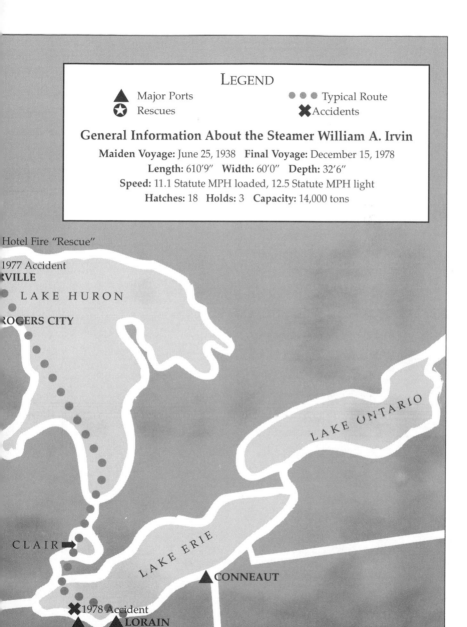

LEGEND

▲ Major Ports   ●●● Typical Route
⭐ Rescues   ✖ Accidents

General Information About the Steamer William A. Irvin

Maiden Voyage: June 25, 1938   Final Voyage: December 15, 1978
Length: 610'9"   Width: 60'0"   Depth: 32'6"
Speed: 11.1 Statute MPH loaded, 12.5 Statute MPH light
Hatches: 18   Holds: 3   Capacity: 14,000 tons

Hotel Fire "Rescue"

1977 Accident
RVILLE

LAKE HURON

ROGERS CITY

LAKE ONTARIO

CLAIR

LAKE ERIE

CONNEAUT

✖ 1978 Accident
SANDUSKY   ▲ LORAIN

At the south end of Lake Michigan, Chicago residents were celebrating Armistice Day as the rapidly-advancing storm tore through Joliet, 30 miles southwest of Chicago. Less than one half-hour later, the cold front passed through Chicago itself, and shortly thereafter, through Gary, Indiana, where a radio tower was blown over (appropriately, for Gary-based station WIND). Lake Superior was already raging with high winds and waves as the IRVIN labored around the Keweenaw Peninsula. Lake Michigan whipped up almost immediately, catching many vessels completely by surprise. While radio was used on ships in 1940, communications were still poor by today's standards. Masters began to change course to bring their vessels into safer waters. The WILLIAM B. DAVOCK and

The IRVIN upbound during the early 1960s.   *(Canal Park Marine Museum collection)*

The size of the Pittsburgh Steamship Company fleet increased greatly between 1906 and 1930 by many nearly-identical vessels. The HENRY STEINBRENNER, above, was built in 1916 and served its first 62 years for U.S. Steel before being sold to George Steinbrenner's Kinsman Lines. Originally named WILLIAM A. McGONAGLE, the 600-footer was renamed in 1986 and served in the grain trade from 1978 through 1989. The vessel is shown above outbound at Duluth on April 16, 1987, with grain. The vessel was scrapped in 1994. *(Author's photo)*

ANNA C. MINCH were not among the lucky vessels; they both foundered not far off the eastern Lake Michigan shore. (When divers found the DAVOCK in 1972, they noticed that the rudder was hard over, indicating that the vessel had likely fallen into a wave trough and fought a losing battle trying to get out.) The Canadian vessel NOVADOC broke in two less than a thousand feet from shore in southern Lake Michigan but too far away for help. Other vessels were grounded in various parts of northern Lake Michigan. Still others, such as the IRVIN's sister ship, the GOVERNOR MILLER, safely reached port and stayed there until winds subsided. After experiencing Lake Superior's worst, the IRVIN finally arrived at the Soo Locks on November 12, late but safe.

Most vessels are usually involved in at least a few accidents during their careers. Fortunately, they do not come as quickly as the lone accident that the CYPRUS, a 440-foot ore boat built in 1907, suffered. The CYPRUS sailed on its maiden voyage in mid-September, 1907. On its fifth trip, during the second week of October, 1907, the CYPRUS was downbound with iron ore in Lake Superior east of Munising, Michigan. Bad weather plagued the entire trip, and on October 11, 1907, the CYPRUS went down, less than a month old. An even more extreme example, although luckily without the same consequences, happened to Pittsburgh Steamship Company's brand-new A.H. FERBERT on its maiden voyage in late August, 1942. When the boat was just a day old, it ran aground in the St. Mary's River and had to go back to the builder's yard in River Rouge, Michigan, for repairs. Although U.S. Steel's vessels, including the IRVIN, have been involved in accidents over the years, the fleet has an outstanding safety record.

On August 26, 1972, the IRVIN was backing away from the North Slip at U.S. Steel's mill in South Chicago. On the way out, the IRVIN backed into a breakwall near the dock, damaging a propeller blade, the rudder, and some hull plating. The vessel was taken to the nearby American Ship Building Company yard, where it spent the next three days undergoing repairs.

The IRVIN just after striking the edge of the Rock Cut in a June 7, 1977, accident. The vessel was not seriously damaged and proceeded underway.
(Howard Weis photo, Canal Park Marine Museum collection)

Another accident occurred on June 7, 1977, while down-bound in the St. Mary's River. A deckhand decided to do some painting in a room. He chipped the old paint off the surface, and used a vacuum cleaner to clean up the paint chips. As soon as he turned on the vacuum cleaner, it tripped an electrical circuit. Up in the pilothouse, the rudder angle indicator began to malfunction just as the boat was making the turn into the Rock Cut. As the name suggests, the channel was carved out of rock, and the sides are nothing but rock walls. The wheelsman thought that river currents were moving the rudder, so he turned the wheel to the left to counteract the current. Unfortunately, the wheelsman was making the turn correctly in the first place, and his "correction" only added to the problem. Since the channel is only a few hundred feet wide, there is little chance to recover from mistakes, and the IRVIN was steered into the side of the Rock Cut. The hull was punctured, but there was no life-threatening damage to the boat. (Nonetheless, the engineers decided that they would have to approve future uses of vacuum cleaners!)

One final accident occurred on what became the IRVIN's last trip with cargo. On December 10, 1978, the IRVIN was approaching the coal dock in Sandusky, Ohio, when it struck a submerged object. The impact was barely noticeable, but it managed to damage some hull plates. The damage again did not require immediate repair so the IRVIN loaded and proceeded to Duluth.

The IRVIN, in the short space of eight months during the mid-1970s, acted in a "Good Samaritan" role twice in quite different situations. On one trip in the fall of 1974, the IRVIN was entering the MacArthur Lock while downbound at Sault Ste. Marie. When any vessel locks through, there is quite a bit of activity on board. The deckhands are called out (regardless of time of day) to go ashore and help handle lines. (From the casual observer's standpoint on shore, it looks like a deckhand taking the boat for a walk.) The Captain takes the front window of the pilothouse (the person navigating the vessel stands by the front window of the pilothouse for an unobstructed view) from the mate, and the mate goes down on deck with walkie-talkies. The mate gives one to the watchman and one to the bosun, and the two of them will assist the mate by giving distances (they use the radios to tell the Captain how far from the side of the lock approach the vessel is.) Meanwhile, the watchman lowers the deckhands down to the dock using the landing boom, or Bosun's chair. It consists of a wooden board attached to a rope suspended from a boom at the forward end of the ship. On deck, a deckhand sits on the board and hangs onto the rope. The watchman swings the boom out over the ship's side, and the Bosun lowers the rope attached to the board down to the dock. The chair is pulled up once the deckhand gets off, and the process is repeated until all the necessary crew is on the dock. One deckhand carries a mail bag and delivers it to the Locks Post Office (and brings back the incoming mail). While all of these people keep busy as the boat approaches the lock, on one trip there was added excitement. One of the people on deck noticed flames coming from the Ojibway Hotel, a Sault Ste. Marie landmark just a block away from the locks. The IRVIN's captain was notified immediately, and he called the Lockmaster to report the blaze. The Lockmaster in turn called the fire department, which quickly put the fire out without injury to anyone or severe property damage. The incident occurred at about 3:00 a.m., and thanks to observant IRVIN crewmembers, ended safely.

The morning of May 31, 1975, was a quiet one as the IRVIN was passing Beaver Island while upbound in Lake Michigan. The next few hours soon turned anxious as a small boat was spotted just after 5:00 a.m. with serious trouble. A 22-foot cabin cruiser, with four people aboard, was taking on some water, and a fuel line was broken. The IRVIN immediately headed for the scene, along with Coast Guard help from shore. At 6:06 a.m., the four people were rescued and brought aboard the IRVIN. Lake waters are still cold in late May and hypothermia can set in within minutes. (Hypothermia is an

The Lower Lake Coal Dock in Sandusky, Ohio, loaded the IRVIN's last cargo on December 10, 1978. This picture of the dock was taken aboard the CASON J. CALLAWAY on August 7, 1990. (Author's photo)

extreme drop in a person's body temperature caused by prolonged, unprotected exposure to severe cold such as cold water. Since a person loses body heat many times faster in water, the body temperature falls fast. If body temperature drops too low, the person dies.) Again, had the IRVIN not been in the right place at the right time, the incident might have turned out quite differently.

By the mid-1970s, there were subtle signs that the IRVIN's sailing career would be ending. The vessel started carrying a wider variety of cargoes, as opposed to predominantly iron ore like the early years of its career. Iron ore was being hauled more often by larger boats in the fleet, which could do the job less expensively. The 1975 season marked the last time the IRVIN's guest rooms and private dining room were regularly used to entertain company guests. The fleet's then-newest boat, the 858-foot ROGER BLOUGH, entered service June 15, 1972, and began carrying the majority of the company's guests in centrally-heated and air-conditioned comfort. In the summer of 1976, U.S. Steel's fleet office decided to open up the IRVIN's guest rooms for use by some of the crew so all officers could have their own rooms. The 1st Mate took one of the guest rooms and one of the 2nd Assistant Engineers moved up forward to get his own room. The memo stated, however, that they needed to be prepared to move out on short notice if guests were carried again.

On Sunday, December 10, 1978, Captain George Fill, Jr. eased the IRVIN away from the Lower Lake Coal Dock in Sandusky, Ohio, with 5,310 tons of coal on board for Duluth. On Friday, December 15, the last of the coal was removed, and the IRVIN proceeded to Fraser Shipyards in Superior, Wisconsin, for the winter. The crew, as usual, laid up the boat for the season, and headed home a few days later. Many of those aboard in 1978 expected that they would return in the spring of 1979 for another sailing season—one which would turn out to be the all-time busiest season for amount of cargo shipped on the Lakes. The IRVIN carried 476,144 tons of cargo in 1978 in 37 trips, one of its top years. Unhappily, the demand for cargoes in 1979 was not quite high enough.

DATE OF LEAVING LOWER PORT _JUNE 10_ 19 _72_ TRIP NO. _8_
CARGO _____ TONS _____

DRAFT, PORT DEPARTURE, FRD _____ P-MID. _____ S-MID. _____ AFT. _____
DRAFT, PORT ARRIVAL, FRD _____ P-MID. _____ S-MID. _____ AFT. _____

DATE OF LEAVING UPPER PORT _JUNE 13,_ 19 _72_
CARGO _±52 Pellets_ TONS _14,019_
DRAFT, PORT DEPARTURE, FRD _22' 06"_ P-MID. _22' 08"_ S-MID. _22' 08"_ AFT. _23' 00"_
DRAFT, PORT ARRIVAL, FRD _22' 08"_ P-MID. _22' 08"_ S-MID. _22' 08"_ AFT. _22' 08"_

FUEL: AMOUNT ON HAND AT END OF PREVIOUS TRIP _So. Chicago_ TONS-GALLONS _80_
AMOUNT PURCHASED _DeTour_ _213_
WHERE PURCHASED
AMOUNT CONSUMED _____ _198_
BALANCE ON HAND - END OF TRIP _So. Chicago_ _95_

GUESTS: MR+MRS J.J. LENNON, JR. (HOST) MR+MRS IVO UMHOEFER MR+MRS PAUL UMHOEFER
MR+MRS ROBERT WALTERMIRE MR+MRS NORMAN STOLTMAN
LENGTH OF TRIP, DAYS _____ HOURS _23"_ (SIGNED) _____ MASTER

BAROMETER	WIND	WEATHER	PLACE TO PLACE	AV. PER MIN.	AV. PER MILE	MILES PER HR.	MILES RUN	REMARKS
								Tug New Mexico -Fwd
								Tug New York - Aft Rd #11
29.67	NNE-22	Pt Cloudy						
29.67	NNE-22	Pt Cloudy						
29.67	NNE-22	Pt Cloudy						⅛₀ 2/200 ¾/220 4/240 -3/250 -4/200 ¾ ⅛/210
29.69	NNE 18	Clear						1200 Time to Engine Room
29.66	NNE-14	Clear						1220 Pumping Out Ballast
								1315 Ballast Pumps Secured
								1315 - 1335 - Steered telemotor
29.66	N-12	Clear						1600 Time To Eng. Rm.
29.65	ENE-10	Clear				115	141	90 100 110 110 220 230 240 240
29.65	NE-6	Clear						2100 Start Senator
								2200 Pumping out -1-2-3-4
29.62	NW-6	Clear						2255 Pump Secured
29.60	Calm	Pt Cloudy						⅛₀ 2/60 ⅝ 4/75 5/160 ⅝/193
								0001 Time to Engine Room
29.60	SxE-12	Pt Cldy						0400 0515 Time To Eng Room Pumping out
29.61	SSW-20	Cldy						0640 1/20 2/30 3/40 4/50 5/100 6/130
29.60	SW-20	Cldy						Pumps off
29.60	SW-20	Cldy						7/120 8/130
29.58	SxW-21	Cloudy						0800 Time To Eng Room
29.54	SW-21	Cloudy						0830 - 0900 Steered Telemotor
29.54	SW-21	Cloudy						
29.52	SW-20	Cloudy						1200 Time To Engine Room
29.52	SW-20	Cloudy						1420 Pumping in Ballast
29.48	SW-20	Cloudy						
29.48	SW-20	Cloudy						
29.48	SW-20	Cloudy						
29.48	WSW-20	Cloudy						

A typical page of the IRVIN's logbook describing trip, cargo, amount, and remarks. On this trip, the IRVIN loaded 14,019 tons of taconite pellets (processed iron ore) in Two Harbors on June 13, 1972.

THE STEAMER WILLIAM A. IRVIN

Made Obsolete

"I used to keep lists of all the old boats that I saw each year. Most of them are all gone now. I remember the IRVIN well— it was one of my favorite ships."

–Cedric Woodard, IRVIN tour guide, former Great Lakes sailor, and lifelong boatwatcher.

On October 31, 1978, the wife of Edwin H. Gott smashed the usual bottle of champagne against the hull of the newest vessel to enter the U. S. Steel fleet. The EDWIN H. GOTT measured 1004 feet long—almost 400 feet longer than the IRVIN. The GOTT's 105-foot width would leave only 30 inches of clearance on each side when the boat passed through the Soo Locks, and the boat would be capable of cargoes in excess of 62,000 tons, or four-and-a-half times the IRVIN's capacity. The GOTT became the most powerful boat on the Great Lakes with twin diesel engines producing a total of 19,500 horsepower. When the GOTT set sail on its maiden voyage February 16, 1979, (the only Great Lakes boat to make a maiden voyage during February), these facts and other reasons, meant that the careers of the IRVIN and other 600-footers were over.

There were five factors which contributed to the end of the IRVIN's career, all economic ones. Most importantly, her

The beautiful 730-foot EDWARD L. RYERSON began setting cargo records soon after it entered service August 4, 1960. This vessel and the EDMUND FITZGERALD held the Great Lakes iron ore cargo record for most of the period from 1960 through 1972. The RYERSON is now an average sized vessel on the Great Lakes. It is shown here downbound with iron ore at Mission Point, St. Mary's River, on July 20, 1988.   *(Author's photo)*

capacity was simply too small by the late 1970s. When the IRVIN entered service, the Great Lakes cargo record was 18,114 tons, set by the ill-fated CARL D. BRADLEY in 1929. There were fewer than 20 boats at the time which were capable of carrying more than the IRVIN's 14,000 tons. While the LEON FRASER became the largest boat on the Lakes on June 21, 1942, snatching the honor from the BRADLEY, its capacity was still under 20,000 tons. The 700-foot ship-length barrier was broken November 4, 1952, when the JOSEPH H. THOMPSON entered service after her conversion from a troop ship used in World

War II. The next large jump in carrying capacity came September 22, 1958, when the EDMUND FITZGERALD entered service. The FITZGERALD, soon to be joined by over 60 boats with nearly identical dimensions, became the largest vessel on the Lakes. The EDWARD L. RYERSON, a vessel similar in size to the FITZGERALD, set an iron ore record of 25,018 tons in August, 1962, and held the record for nearly three years. In 1966, the FITZGERALD became the first vessel to carry over 26,000 tons in one load, and it continued to set records throughout the 1960s. The FITZGERALD's last record load was 27,402 tons—a capacity nearly twice that of the IRVIN—loaded in

The GEORGE A. STINSON is one of 13 vessels at least 1000 feet long which currently operate on the Great Lakes. Vessels like the IRVIN could not compete with the STINSON's 60,000 ton capacity after it entered service in August, 1978. This photo shows the STINSON upbound at Mission Point, St. Mary's River, on September 30, 1989.   (Author's photo)

Silver Bay on August 10, 1969. At the start of the 1970s, vessels in the 600-foot class were still busy carrying iron ore—there were even a few vessels left under 450 feet long. However, the STEWART J. CORT—the first of the new 1000-footers—put the records set by the 730-foot vessels to rest for good during the first week of May, 1972, when it loaded over 49,300 tons on its first trip. Not long thereafter, all of the sub-500 foot vessels not engaged in some special trade were retired, and some 600-footers also sailed their last. By the end of the 1970s, the 730-footers had become average size vessels, less than 10 years after

The MYRON C. TAYLOR is the smallest of the American vessels currently being used for bulk cargo on the Great Lakes, other than tankers or cement carriers. Only several modifications, including conversion to a self-unloader and receiving a diesel engine have kept this 1929-vintage, 603-foot vessel in service. This photo shows the TAYLOR outbound from Toledo on June 25, 1990, as it passes its larger fleetmate, the CASON J. CALLAWAY.
(Author's photo)

An advantage of a self-unloader over a straight-deck vessel like the IRVIN is illustrated here in this photograph taken aboard the CASON J. CALLAWAY on August 17, 1990. The CALLAWAY's self-unloading boom is extended over the shore at the Marblehead dock on the Rouge River in Detroit as the vessel unloads limestone. The "dock" is nothing more than a recessed area in the river, and the vessel is a fair distance away from the shore. Vessels like the IRVIN are incapable of delivering to such docks, and this flexibility (as well as reduced unloading time) has made self-unloaders the vessel of choice. The CALLAWAY spent just over six hours discharging this cargo, in excess of 22,000 tons. (Author's photo)

they were setting records. Many vessels during the 1960s and 1970s were lengthened by adding 72-, 96-, or even 120-foot midsections to them. These boats were cut in two in a shipyard, the sections pulled apart, and the pre-fabricated midsection floated into place between the two original sections. The entire boat was carefully realigned and welded together. Even if the IRVIN had been lengthened, it would have added only a couple thousand tons to the capacity, which would not have earned enough to pay for the costly shipyard work. As of the 2000 shipping season, the smallest vessel being used by the American Great Lakes fleets, other than cement carriers and tankers, was U.S. Steel's 603-foot MYRON C. TAYLOR, built in 1929. If size were the only factor affecting vessel longevity, the TAYLOR would likely not be around today. However, it received a life-preserving addition in 1956 which the IRVIN and many other vessels did not.

The TAYLOR was converted to a self-unloader during 1956 at Sturgeon Bay, Wisconsin. Self-unloaders first made their appearance on the Lakes in 1901, when the HENNEPIN was converted to a self-unloader. The WYANDOTTE became the first vessel constructed as a self-unloader, in 1908. They were initially designed for carrying limestone. Even in the 1950s, there were still only a handful of self-unloaders on the Lakes. Self-unloaders are incredibly versatile boats, since they don't depend on shoreside unloading equipment. For example, when the Mackinac Bridge was being built in the mid-1950s, self-unloaders were used to haul the limestone from nearby Drummond Island to the construction site. The self-unloader would tie up to the partially completed caissons, swing their booms out, and limestone would stream off and settle into a strong foundation for the massive bridge support piers. During the 1960s, a few Canadian fleets began converting some of their vessels to self-unloaders, and American fleets began doing so in earnest in the 1970s. (In fact, the last new American non-self-unloading vessels were the PIONEER CHALLENGER, WALTER A. STERLING, LEON FALK, JR., and PAUL H. CARNAHAN, which were converted into ore boats from old ocean tankers in 1961. The first two have been converted to self-unloaders and are now sailing under different names; the other two were not converted and were scrapped in the mid-1980s.)

Besides their versatility, self-unloaders unload much faster than shoreside systems. For example, U.S. Steel's CASON J. CALLAWAY, with a 25,000 ton capacity, took about 17 hours to unload a cargo in 1981 before its conversion. The following winter, it received its self-unloading system at Fraser Shipyards in Superior, Wisconsin. Now, the vessel requires only about six hours for unloading—a nearly half-day reduction each trip which adds up during a season. Vessels similar in size to the IRVIN have been converted to self-unloaders before. However, conversions in the early 1980s cost up to $13 million, a figure which seemed hard to justify for a vessel which originally cost only $1,557,000 in 1938 and had other factors which made it obsolete.

Another such factor involves the IRVIN's speed. Records from the late 1960s show that the IRVIN and sister GOVERNOR MILLER were the two slowest boats U.S. Steel owned. Even their other 600-foot class boats, some of which go back as far as 1906, would manage a few tenths of a mile per hour faster (not a big difference, but it adds up over the entire season). Significant increases in speed from the 11 to 12 MPH range did not occur until the WILFRED SYKES entered service in April of 1950. The SYKES, in addition to being the largest boat on the Lakes at that time, was the fastest as well, with a speed of nearly 16 MPH with a full load. Then, in 1951, four vessels entered service which were even quicker. The CLIFFS VICTORY, a former World War II Victory-class ship, and the TROY H. BROWNING, TOM M. GIRDLER, and CHARLES M.

When it entered service April 19, 1950, the 678-foot WILFRED SYKES was the largest ore boat on the Great Lakes. Now it is among the smallest vessels used in the iron ore trade. This photo shows the SYKES outbound through the Duluth piers with a load of iron ore on August 23, 1988.
(Author's photo)

WHITE, all former C-4 class ocean vessels constructed at the end of World War II, were converted into ore boats. It is disputed which one was the fastest (the CHARLES M. WHITE made the 382-mile trip across Lake Superior in 17 hours one trip in May, 1953, under full load), but all four eclipsed the SYKES and the other vessels. Most future vessels on the American side were equipped with horsepower sufficient to at least tie the SYKES' standard.

When the 1000-footers entered service, they too were designed for a speed in the 15 MPH range, although some had a little bit more power. U.S. Steel's ROGER BLOUGH is capable of 17.5 MPH under full load. Since the CLIFFS VICTORY and the former C-4 conversions were sold for scrap in the early 1980s, the BLOUGH holds the honor as fastest on the American side of the Lakes. Several Canadian vessels are capable of similar speeds. On a trip-by-trip basis, the fastest vessels on the Lakes have made round trips in five days, while the IRVIN was lucky to make a trip in under seven days. If the IRVIN sailed a 245-day season (eight months, which was about the longest it ever ran in one year), it could make 35 such trips. A boat needing only five days from Duluth to the Lower Lakes and back would make 49 trips in the same period. But these faster vessels tend to run longer seasons as well, which means even more trips. For example, the ROGER BLOUGH was one of the pioneers in the year-round navigation experiments of the mid-1970s, and it would regularly run in excess of 300-day seasons. Vessels like the IRVIN, with weak horsepower ratings, would be among the first to have trouble in ice, as Patrick Kennedy and Herbert Thorson testified earlier. Many older vessels have been repowered with higher horsepower engines, enabling them to travel at greater speed and make more trips per year. Vessels such as the MYRON C. TAYLOR, CALCITE II, and the KINSMAN ENTERPRISE (the KINSMAN ENTERPRISE is the former HARRY COULBY, once the Great Lakes iron ore record holder) are three examples of late-1920s vessels which were repowered many years ago and sailing in the 1990s as a result. But both the TAYLOR and the CALCITE II are self-unloaders, and the KINSMAN ENTERPRISE is an ideal vessel for use in the domestic grain trade. The IRVIN had relatively low cubic capacity in its holds and would not have been an effective grain hauler. Also, fuel prices indicate that high speed is impor-

The IRVIN downbound in the St. Mary's River with a full load near the Soo Locks during 1969. *(Institute for Great Lakes Research collection)*

tant only up to a certain point, so even repowering the IRVIN would not necessarily have made it a competitive carrier.

When it was retired in 1978, the IRVIN was one of a dwindling number of coal burning vessels on the Great Lakes. Steam-powered boats burning #6 fuel oil became popular in the 1950s, and after they did, many previous coal burners were converted to burn the heavy oil. Even some of the new coal burners built in the 1950s, such as the EDMUND FITZGERALD and the ERNEST T. WEIR (now the COURTNEY BURTON) were converted to oil. There is only one coal burner left running on the Lakes—the car-ferry BADGER, built in 1952, which makes runs between Manitowoc, Wisconsin, and Ludington, Michigan.

The ultimate factor which made the IRVIN obsolete—its crew size—was somewhat related to the fuel used. The IRVIN usually had a crew of 32, with extra galley crew on board for the summer guests. Most vessels on the Lakes now have a crew size in the mid-20s, while some of the newer tug-barge combinations have an even smaller crew. In the IRVIN's engine department, there would typically be an assistant engineer, an oiler, and two firemen or coalpassers on duty at any time. The firemen and coalpassers would clean out the fireboxes, monitor the water level in the boilers, and handle other tasks related to the boiler room and the fuel. On oil-fired steam vessels, there is usually just an engineer and an oiler on duty for each watch, with additional help during the day for cleaning, painting, and other maintenance work. The boiler room crew has been replaced by a computer to control the fuel-air mixture, monitor water level, and handle other boiler functions. Again, while a conversion to oil fuel and installing automated boiler controls may have helped the IRVIN in two areas, it still remained too small and too slow to compete against ore boats five times its size. Since the IRVIN had to rely on shoreside unloading systems, many of which had been dismantled, the vessel had no flexibility when compared to a self-unloader. In short, by the late 1970s the IRVIN's useful days as a cargo-carrying vessel were over, caused by increased emphasis on shipping cargo for as low a rate as possible.

By Jody Aho

IRVIN Cargo History

The number of times the IRVIN visited a port to load and the number of cargoes of each type loaded are listed year-by-year. Most of the data comes from a cargo register for the Pittsburgh Steamship Company covering 1942 through 1971, while the remainder comes from IRVIN logbooks and vessel traffic listings in the Duluth News-Tribune, the Detroit Free Press, the Detroit News, the Cleveland Plain Dealer, and the Cleveland News.

Year	Duluth	Two Harbors	Calcite Port (Rogers City)	Dolomite (Cedarville)	Total Trips	Ore	Stone	Coal	Slag	Remark
1938	9	11	0	0	21	20	0	0	1	(1)
1939	20	5	2	0	29	27	2	0	0	(2)
1940	14	15	2	0	31	29	2	0	0	
1941	24	11	1	0	36	35	1	0	0	
1942	23	11	3	0	37	34	3	0	0	
1943	14	16	3	0	33	30	3	0	0	
1944	12	20	3	0	35	32	3	0	0	
1945	21	10	4	0	35	31	4	0	0	
1946	10	18	0	0	28	28	0	0	0	
1947	19	14	0	0	33	33	0	0	0	
1948	23	10	5	0	38	33	5	0	0	
1949	18	9	1	0	28	27	1	0	0	
1950	21	8	3	0	32	29	3	0	0	
1951	20	14	4	0	38	34	4	0	0	
1952	11	13	3	0	27	24	3	0	0	
1953	15	19	4	0	38	32	4	0	0	
1954	7	18	4	0	31	27	4	0	0	(2)
1955	14	15	8	0	37	29	8	0	0	
1956	7	15	5	1	28	22	6	0	0	
1957	12	17	0	0	30	29	0	1	0	(3)
1958	8	14	8	2	32	22	10	0	0	
1959	5	9	1	1	16	14	2	0	0	
1960	7	21	0	2	30	28	2	0	0	
1961	9	17	1	0	27	26	1	0	0	
1962	4	21	2	2	29	25	4	0	0	
1963	26	0	3	0	29	26	3	0	0	
1964	27	0	5	4	36	27	9	0	0	
1965	26	0	0	1	29	26	2	1	0	(4)
1966	22	8	1	2	33	30	3	0	0	
1967	22	3	3	3	33	25	6	2	0	(5)
1968	23	6	1	6	36	29	7	0	0	
1969	20	7	3	3	34	28	6	0	0	(6)
1970	23	8	3	1	35	31	4	0	0	
1971	21	2	1	3	27	23	4	0	0	
1972	19	6	10	2	38	26	12	0	0	(6)
1973	8	23	1	5	37	31	6	0	0	
1974	15	14	4	0	37	29	4	2	2	(7)
1975	18	5	2	0	26	23	2	0	1	(8)
1976	20	3	2	2	33	23	4	6	0	(9)
1977	13	0	0	0	13	13	0	0	0	
1978	21	2	4	4	37	23	8	6	0	(10)
Total	**671**	**438**	**110**	**44**	**1292**	**1115**	**155**	**18**	**4**	

Other loading ports with total number of trips: Sandusky, 7; Toledo, 6; Ashland, 4: South Chicago, 3; Buffington, 3; Superior, 2; Ashtabula, 2; Drummond Island, 1; Conneaut, 1.

(1) Includes one load of slag from South Chicago.
(2) Includes two loads of ore from Ashland, Wisconsin.
(3) Includes one load of coal from Toledo.
(4) Includes one load of coal from South Chicago and one load of stone from Drummond Island, Michigan.
(5) Includes two loads of coal from Toledo.
(6) Includes one load of iron ore from Superior.

(7) Includes two loads of slag from Buffington, Indiana; one load of coal from Conneaut, Ohio; and one load of coal from South Chicago.
(8) Includes one load of slag from Buffington.
(9) Includes four loads of coal from Sandusky, Ohio, and two loads of coal from Ashtabula, Ohio.
(10) Includes three loads of coal from Toledo and three of coal from Sandusky.

1978-1986: The Uncertain Years

*"There were piles of junk everywhere
and no paint left in the engine room.
But being an ex-sailor, I could see the
potential."*

–Bob Hom, Director of Operations for the Duluth
Entertainment Convention Center, present owners
of the IRVIN, recalling his first visit aboard the
IRVIN during its long lay-up.

The 1979 shipping season became the busiest in Great Lakes history in terms of total cargo carried—215 million tons. Shipyards around the Great Lakes were busy—two new 1000-footers in 1979, two others due in the fall of 1980, and two more due early in 1981, along with a handful of smaller vessels. With newer, larger, and faster vessels coming on the scene, the small, slow 600-footers of the earlier decades of the century began ringing up "FINISHED WITH ENGINES" for the last time. In 1982, the tonnage total for the Great Lakes had fallen by over a third from the 1979 record. The employment scene of the early 1980s resembled that exactly fifty years earlier. Unemployment rates eventually reached double digits nationwide and even higher levels in Minnesota's ore mining communities. The economy entered a deep recession and with it went the public's confidence in

Contrary to the sign (lower left), the IRVIN's career was not at a dead end, though many thought otherwise when this photo was taken in 1982.
(C. Patrick Labadie photo, Canal Park Marine Museum collection)

spending money to buy new cars or appliances—products made from steel made by the mills which received the iron ore carried by the Great Lakes vessels.

The former Columbia Transportation Division of Oglebay Norton Company retired several vessels in 1979; another major hauler, Cleveland-Cliffs, saw a dramatic reduction in business in 1980 (and the end of the fleet in 1984); and many other companies, including U.S. Steel— known as USS Great Lakes Fleet as of June, 1981—at the end of the 1981 season reduced their rosters also. The IRVIN, laid up at a remote dock in West Duluth (it was towed to various places around the harbor during its lay-up), soon had company from other fleetmates which, for the same reasons as the IRVIN, could no longer compete with the new boats. After 1979, 1980, and 1981—three strong years—the 1982 season saw some of the lowest tonnage totals since the 1930s, and the fleets were desperate to haul anything. USS Great Lakes Fleet even found some grain cargoes to keep the BENJAMIN F. FAIRLESS running during 1982 before it, too, was sent to join laid-up fleetmates in West Duluth, all with uncertain futures.

The 1983 season saw little improvement, and some of the boats laid up in West Duluth and in other places around the Lakes were sold for scrap. One of the IRVIN's sisters, the JOHN HULST, met its fate in Thunder Bay in 1983; some of the older boats were towed away that year. But the IRVIN, docked on the inside of its slip, with boats to the side of it and behind it, was safe for the moment.

Meanwhile, some groups in the Duluth area had other visions other than scrapping for the fleet of ore boats laid up in the harbor. The IRVIN, the most glamorous of the bunch because of the guest rooms and other interior fittings, began receiving the most attention. Ideas as diverse as meeting rooms in the cargo holds, a shipboard restaurant, and even a casino to be run by the nearby Fond du Lac Indian Reservation, were being tossed around. In June, 1983, Duluth Mayor John Fedo was involved in discussions with USS Great Lakes Fleet officials concerning the IRVIN's future use. Ideas were also underway for a major expansion to the Arena-Auditorium on Duluth's waterfront, including a new convention center and hotel. Julia and Caroline Marshall, two sisters who have played a key role in many local projects over the years, expressed their interest. Could the IRVIN somehow fit in as part of the new convention center? A series of letters were exchanged between the mayor's office and USS Great Lakes Fleet, but at the end of 1983, there was still nothing definite, except that the idea of a shipboard casino was ruled out since there were too many delays and the Fond du Lac Reservation felt that other, land-based sites would bring more traffic.

The following year again saw little improvement, and more laid-up vessels were meeting scrapper torches. The IRVIN was still safe, as alternative uses for it continued to be explored. One question which became apparent involved the IRVIN's location in the harbor. Its lay-up berth, plagued by high grass, shrubs, and poor access, was obviously unsuitable. The Arena-Auditorium, downtown, was four miles away, and there were several spots near there which could serve as the boat's home. One of the early favorites was a location in Duluth's Bayfront Park, which in 1984 was still a mostly underutilized open field adjacent to busy industrial property. Plans for an $18 million Lake Superior Center were proposed, which could include the IRVIN as well as a museum, a marina for small boats, and a freshwater aquarium. The dock behind the Arena-Auditorium was already well-developed structurally, but it was in an exposed location which left it vulnerable to poor weather and the remote chance of severe damage by a runaway outbound vessel with steering gear failure. There was also a slip on the east side of the Arena which was used in the 1930s by package freighters and remained part of an adjacent coal dock until it closed in 1964 to make way for the new Arena-Auditorium complex. Despite these ideas, the IRVIN completed its sixth year of lay-up with no foreseeable future besides staying at its lay-up berth. 1985 marked the fourth poor year in a row for Great Lakes shipping. While tonnage figures were creeping upward, they were still far behind the glory years of 1979, 1980, and 1981, which were still fresh in everyone's memory.

The early part of 1986 saw increased activity for the IRVIN and its future. The Minnesota Legislature was considering a $16 million appropriation for Duluth's new convention center, including money for possible purchase and renovation of the IRVIN. Meanwhile, the Duluth State Convention Center Board, the agency overseeing the Arena-Auditorium, was debating the purchase of the IRVIN. On April 15, 1986, the Convention Center Board voted unanimously to buy the IRVIN for scrap value—$110,000—and renovate the vessel. Bids on the renovation were taken over the next few weeks, and early in May, Fraser Shipyards of Superior was awarded the approximately $255,000 contract. On May 12, 1986, a cold, foggy day, two of the IRVIN's former fleetmates were moved aside, as two tugs eased the IRVIN out of the slip it had occupied for seven years. The tow made its way past the Duluth Missabe and Iron Range ore docks, (where the IRVIN had loaded 671 times over its forty-year sailing career) and into Howard's Pocket (a small branch of the Duluth-Superior harbor), then into Fraser Shipyards, and finally the drydock.

An extensive work list was ready for the vessel, and the deadline for completion was Monday, June 23, 1986. The majority of the work included sandblasting, priming, and repainting practically every surface on the boat, but numerous other tasks were specified as well. To prevent possibility of flooding, all under-the-waterline hull openings had plates welded over them. The brass railings in the engine room were cleaned and polished for the first time in nearly a decade. Other minor repairs to the engine room were performed, so the IRVIN would remain the "triumph in safety" that the boat's namesake had proclaimed almost fifty years before. Officials from the IRVIN's new owners, the Duluth Arena-Auditorium (to become the Duluth Entertainment Convention Center in the summer of 1988) made frequent visits to Fraser Shipyards to view the progress.

"I made it to the shipyard a couple of times a week," remembers Bob Hom, Director of Operations for the Duluth Entertainment Convention Center and former deckhand on the steamer ARMCO in 1970. "It was neat being in the drydock, being right underneath the boat. I've got a picture of me standing on the rudder shoe."

While the IRVIN was being readied for the public, the Arena-Auditorium officials were developing a staff to work on the vessel. On May 28, Roy Harnish, the Arena-Auditorium's Director of Promotion and Public Relations, was named

The IRVIN is being eased out of Fraser Shipyards by tugs SIOUX and DAKOTA on June 17, 1986, on its way to a new career. (Tim Slattery photo, Duluth Entertainment Convention Center collection)

Director of Tours and Promotion for the IRVIN. Harnish immediately sought volunteers who were interested in the IRVIN or Great Lakes ships in general, former Great Lakes sailors, and people with technical knowledge to work as tour guides, interpreters, and on additional renovation projects on board.

The shipyard work was completed ahead of schedule and, on the sunny morning of Tuesday, June 17, 1986, the North

The IRVIN is being backed out of Fraser Shipyards on June 17, 1986, en route to the temporary berth behind the Duluth Arena. *(Tim Slattery photo, Duluth Entertainment Convention Center collection)*

American Towing Company tugs SIOUX and DAKOTA backed the IRVIN out of Fraser Shipyard. The tugs turned the vessel, and the tow proceeded under the Blatnik Bridge, around Rice's Point, past Duluth's many grain elevators and the scrap dock with some of the IRVIN's former fleetmates awaiting their doom, and to the dock behind the Arena-Auditorium. This dock served as a temporary home while Minnesota Slip, the final berth for the IRVIN on the east side of the Arena, was being repaired. The IRVIN arrived behind the Arena just after noon to be greeted by a crowd of spectators. The following day, Roy Harnish gave a tour to a number of interested volunteers as additional refurbishing was done in the engine room and other areas. One final hitch was thrown into the tour plans; there was a slight delay obtaining the necessary liability insurance, and the IRVIN's June 21 opening was postponed one week. The soon-to-be IRVIN tour guides met during that week to polish up the tour narration, discuss the work schedule, and see to last minute details. Everyone eagerly awaited June 28, Opening Day!

ACKNOWLEDGEMENT

The staff of the WILLIAM A. IRVIN and the Duluth Entertainment Convention Center gratefully acknowledge the efforts of Robert Heimbach. As a member of the Board of Directors of the Duluth Entertainment Convention Center, Bob was instrumental in the acquisition of the WILLIAM A. IRVIN by the Duluth Entertainment Convention Center. Bob's hard work and dedication to the WILLIAM A. IRVIN has made the retired ore carrier what it is today.

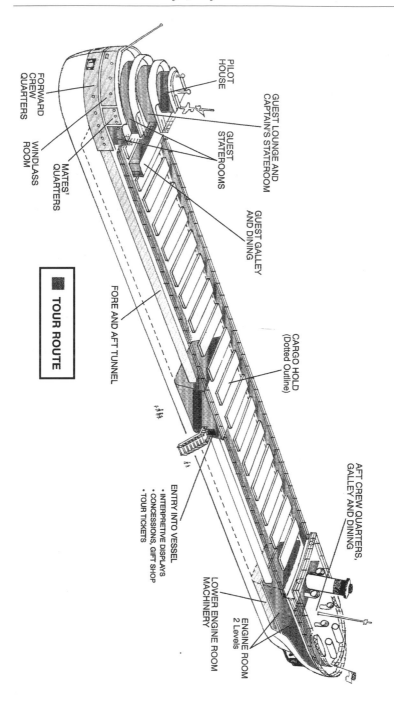

PILOT HOUSE

GUEST LOUNGE AND CAPTAIN'S STATEROOM

FORWARD CREW QUARTERS

GUEST STATEROOMS

WINDLASS ROOM

MATES' QUARTERS

GUEST GALLEY AND DINING

FORE AND AFT TUNNEL

TOUR ROUTE

CARGO HOLD (Dotted Outline)

ENTRY INTO VESSEL
• INTERPRETIVE DISPLAYS
• CONCESSIONS, GIFT SHOP
• TOUR TICKETS

AFT CREW QUARTERS, GALLEY AND DINING

LOWER ENGINE ROOM MACHINERY

ENGINE ROOM 2 Levels

Open for Tours

"She was the Queen of the Lakes and so shall she remain for the rest of her days."

—Captain John J. McDonough, the captain who brought the IRVIN into Minnesota Slip in 1986 and who made the above final entry in the ship's log on October 15, 1986.

On Saturday morning, June 28, 1986, the IRVIN staff reported for the first day of public tours. No one knew what to expect, even IRVIN director Roy Harnish commented the day before, "If we have 10,000 people lined up out there tomorrow, I don't know what we'll do." With partly cloudy skies and mild temperatures, weather certainly would not keep people away. While a crowd of 10,000 didn't flood the ticket booth that morning, a long line had started forming by 9:30, and there were easily enough people to fill the first four tours. Tickets were sold, and the first tour was getting ready to leave. At 10:00 a.m., the chain at the bottom of the stairs was opened, and the first 22 guests climbed up the stairs and into the engine room.

The IRVIN's popularity quickly spread, and before two weeks were out the IRVIN had hosted its 10,000th visitor. While many interested people volunteered from the start to give tours, soon several new tour guides were recruited from the "redcoats" (ushers) in the Duluth Arena-Auditorium because business was stronger than expected. Meanwhile, the original volunteers were busy preparing more sections of the boat for tours. Within a few weeks of opening day, a motor generator set was running in the engine room to give visitors a somewhat quieter version of the noise in an operating engine room. The shuffleboard court (between hatches 5 and 6) was repainted and shuffleboard sticks awaited on deck.

The IRVIN's temporary berth behind the Arena provided its share of challenges and presented reasons to support the move into Minnesota Slip as soon as possible. On days with strong northeast winds, the vessel developed a slight but noticeable roll, and on one occasion the postcards in the outdoor gift shop were blown into the bay. Parking was a block away, and the vessel seemed well-hidden from people traveling through downtown Duluth. Late on a Friday night in September, a storm with 40 MPH northeast winds blew through the area, breaking the IRVIN loose from the dock. The problem was quickly discovered, and tugs (and "linehandlers" from the Arena-Auditorium) were called to work through the night to secure the boat. The following day became one of the boat's busiest ever as the previous night's events attracted curiosity. With the stormy fall season just starting, the IRVIN needed better shelter soon. On Monday morning, October 13, the tugs were dispatched again, those interested and available tour guides reported aboard, and Captain John J. McDonough —off from his regular job as captain of U.S. Steel's CASON J. CALLAWAY—came aboard to guide the IRVIN on its short, final trip into its new home. The IRVIN had no power of its own to assist the tow, and it was not until after lunch that the vessel was finally tied up. The IRVIN finished out the 1986 season on Sunday, November 2.

Since 1986, the WILLIAM A. IRVIN has provided visitors with a chance to see a Great Lakes vessel on the inside. The IRVIN crew has always strived to make each person's visit an educational yet entertaining experience. The boat was a pioneer in its day, named after a triumphant, self-educated industry leader. The boat served as a dependable carrier for 40 years, serving a dual public relations and workhorse role throughout much of that time. The IRVIN managed to escape the fate of so many of its unlucky fleetmates during the 1980s, and it has since grown to become a major part of Duluth's waterfront.

In 1992, WDSE-TV, the local public television station, prepared a segment on the IRVIN for their weekly "Album" series focusing on local history. Throughout the rest of the summer and fall, preparations were underway for *Haunted Tours*, a promotion for Halloween. The *Haunted Tours* were designed in part for fundraising for the University of Minnesota-Duluth Theatre Department, and the local food shelf. Actors, props, and technical assistance was provided by UMD, and the IRVIN staff sold tickets and provided crowd control. The idea was a smashing success, as 15,000 people visited the IRVIN during the nine-evening run. A creative promotion plan reached large numbers, and early visitors spread the word to family and friends. The *Haunted Tours* continue each Halloween.

With over 15 years in its new career, the IRVIN crew hopes to give visitors a glimpse of life on a boat for years to come.

BIBLIOGRAPHY

"Big Freighter Ready for Dip," Detroit News, November 10, 1937.

Boyer, Dwight. Strange Adventures of the Great Lakes. New York: Dodd, Mead, Inc., 1974.

Duluth News-Tribune, June 26, 27, 28, 29, 1938; November 3, 1940; November 11, 12, 13, 1940; January 26, 29, 1984; March 21, 1986; April 15, 1986; April 29, 1986; July 14, 1990.

Great Lakes Ships We Remember III. Cleveland: Freshwater Press, Inc., 1994.

Greenwood, John O. Namesakes of the '80's. Cleveland: Freshwater Press, Inc., 1980.

Greenwood, John O. Namesakes of the Lakes. Cleveland: Freshwater Press, Inc., 1970.

Hemming, Robert J. Gales of November: The Sinking of the EDMUND FITZGERALD. Chicago: Contemporary Books, Inc., 1981.

Hull 811, WILLIAM A. IRVIN. Lorain, Ohio: American Ship Building Company, 1938.

King, Franklin A. "Two Harbors: Minnesota's First Iron Ore Port." Nor'Easter, September-October 1984.

Lake Carriers Association Annual Report, 1929.

Lake Carriers Association Annual Report, 1932.

Lake Carriers Association Annual Report, 1979.

Manse, Thomas. Know Your Ships. Sault Ste. Marie, Michigan: Marine Publishing Company, 1985.

"New Ship Hits the Water", Toledo Blade, November 11, 1937.

New York Times, January 2, 1952.

Redford, C.I. "Along the Waterfront", Toronto Evening Telegram, November 11, 1937.

Rubin, Lawrence A. Mighty Mac. Detroit: Wayne State University Press, 1979.

Skillings Mining Review, November 20, 1937.

Superior Evening Telegram, October 11, 1974.

Who's Who In America. Chicago: The A.N. Marquis Company, 1950.

The CASON J. CALLAWAY is an example of an average-sized boat on the Great Lakes today. It was built in 1952 as a 647-foot straight deck vessel. In 1974, it was lengthened 120 feet at Fraser Shipyards in Superior. In 1982, the CALLAWAY was converted to a self-unloader by the same shipyard. It is powered by steam turbines totalling 7000 horsepower. The vessel is shown here outbound Duluth piers on September 8, 1987. This is the vessel the author sailed on for 2-1/2 months in 1990.   (Author's photo)

About the Author

Jody Aho is a lifelong Duluth resident and boatwatcher, and has worked as a tour guide aboard the WILLIAM A. IRVIN since its 1986 opening. He sailed one summer as a deck cadet aboard the CASON J. CALLAWAY while attending the Great Lakes Maritime Academy. While he no longer sails the Great Lakes, he does maintain an active interest in Great Lakes ships. He has been a member of the Lake Superior Marine Museum Association since 1983 and served on its Board of Directors from 1995 to 2000. He volunteers as "Weather Watcher" for KBJR-TV in Duluth. He is a graduate of the University of Minnesota-Duluth with a Bachelor of Applied Science Degree in secondary education.